MAYBE TODAY

THOUGHTS, PRAYERS AND SMILES

WITH
TONY MILES

CWR

For Frances, Hannah and Jonathan
– I am very proud of you all.
May you continue to grow in your Christian faith
with hope and love.

With thanksgiving to God for the lives of
Rob Frost, Donald English and Chris Bard:
three men of God, now in Glory, who have
significantly influenced my life, faith and ministry.

'As long as you live, keep learning how to live.'
Seneca – Roman philosopher, dramatist, poet and statesman
(c. 4 BC – AD 65)

'Tony has the most fun-loving, faith-filled, fertile mind of anyone I know. I nick his ideas all the time and he doesn't seem to mind a bit! I used to think "How on earth does he manage to stay so positive?" Now I've read this book I know.'
Andrew Graystone
Director, Churches' Media Council

'Stacked full of Tony's profound insight and peppered with prayers, readings and a good dose of humour, *Maybe Today* is a call to pursue and live for God! A brilliant resource!'
Andy Frost
Director, Share Jesus International

'Tony is a fantastic communicator. In this book he makes the Bible come to life with real relevance. It's an easy read and a must read!'
Peter Kerridge
CEO, Premier Christian Radio

'In broadcasting, preaching and writing Tony Miles has a great gift of communicating God's love and truth in a clear and interesting way. In this gem of a book Tony's thoughts and prayers are set alongside the wisdom of the ages to provide a great resource for everyday Christian living. A great read and a great gift to pass on!'
Martin Turner
Superintendent, Methodist Central Hall, Westminster

'This is not just another "daily reading book" … but a maybe today book! Tony helps us to understand and smile at self-imposed pressures, and exchange them for a God-centred life lived in the knowledge of how much we are cherished by the Father.

Being in the process of "starting again" after Rob's death my day-by-day prayer is: God's place … God's work … God's relationships … God's timing … God's power …'

Jacqui Frost
Director, Lantern Arts Centre

'In our fast paced world comes a collection of devotions designed to make us stop, reflect, and find time to "peel the carrots". No religious speak here – just an honest look at life, faith and love through the eyes of an honest man.'

Mike Rayson,
Australian Singer/Songwriter and Pastor, Nashville TN

'Inspirational reflections! I love how real and down-to-earth they are … who could believe some of the situations Tony has found himself in?! All written with a random humour that only the Reverend Miles possesses!'

Lizzie Crow
Presenter, Premier Christian Radio

CONTENTS

FOREWORD

In one of the introductions to *Maybe Today*, Tony Miles draws our attention to the consequences of split-second decisions. Like many of us, I know what it means to decide quickly and then ponder on how my life might have been if I'd chosen another path. However, I think much less about how my split-second decisions affect others, especially the decisions that go unnoticed .

Yet there's something sobering about considering the impact of the insignificant, ongoing, minutiae of our daily lives. As we rush around, focusing on the big and important, what, or *who* do we overlook? How do we become more like God, in the detail, when our minds are on the big things?

This beautifully executed book provides a gentle daily nudge that encourages us to always examine our actions, in relation to the template laid out by God. But it doesn't bully us into doing so – in fact the title, *Maybe Today*, says it all. This book is pressure-free. Which is great news if, like me, you can feel guilty about not doing what you want to do, and guilt-ridden by what you do.

Some of the other devotionals – many brilliant – can unwittingly feed our guilt, especially for me the ones that are presented in date form. Just the dates themselves can feel like judgmental reminders of all the days I've missed, which is a sure-fire way of inspiring someone like me to give up!

Fortunately, this thoughtful, warm book has none of that. Tony truly understands what many of our lives look like, and so hasn't created unrealistic expectations in the following pages. Instead he's cleverly produced a book that's pragmatic about the challenges of modern life, whilst at the same time remaining utterly faithful to God.

The style of *Maybe Today* – a neat blend of humour and heart – captures the character of Tony Miles, which is passionately compassionate. It's in Tony's DNA to care about people, to have a ridiculously naff sense of humour (Jonathan and Hannah I agree with you; your dad really is random), and above all to have a burning hunger to live more and more like God, coupled with an urgency to share this great God with others.

I highly commend Tony and I highly recommend *Maybe Today*. It reminds me of an Advent Crown stacked with goodies you want to devour in one go but know you'll get more benefit from savouring one succulent bite-size a day.

So if you're looking for a regular injection of spiritual nourishment in a practical, engaging and contemporary way then this is the book for you.

Oh by the way, just in case I've not made myself clear, I really love this book!

Diane Louise Jordan
TV presenter, author, corporate speaker and patron of many charities

PREFACE
BEFORE YOU READ THIS BOOK

A German proverb says, 'No honest man ever repented of his honesty.'

- *Are you perfect?* If so, there's no point in reading any further because you obviously won't need this book. Beware though! There's just the possibility that, because of your claim, you might not be as flawless as you think. So, just in case, try swallowing some pride and read on.
- *Are you intellectually superior?* If so, you might be better off grappling with a more weighty academic tome. You know the type of book. *Maybe Today* is not intended to be a work of systematic theology, but a random collection of devotional material.
- *Are you in total control and never harassed?* If so, what's it like? I admire you. Perhaps you could give *Maybe Today* to someone like me: a simple soul who wants to be like Jesus, but often feels terribly unworthy, struggling with what it means to be a Christian in practice in this stressful ever-changing world; someone who is utterly amazed that God transforms the ordinary into the extraordinary to further the work of His kingdom.
- *If you are none of the above, then read on!* However, don't get too excited, this is not a 'How To' book with all the answers on how to be holy. Rather, *Maybe Today* asks some questions and will hopefully help you to reflect, pray and smile too. I trust you will find God speaking to you as you turn these pages, just as I found the Holy Spirit whispering to me.

Jesus said, 'But when he, the Spirit of truth, comes, he will guide you into all truth' (John 16:13a).

LIGHTEN UP

Is it just me? I worry that Christians take themselves far too seriously. It's a cliché, but Jesus wants us to be *born again*, not *bored again*. It's no wonder some people are put off Christianity when they look at the faces and lives of some of God's people. He loves us all, despite the fact that our lives are not always as attractive as they should be. The deep joy in some Christians seems to have sunk so deep that it can't be seen! I'm not advocating people adopt a fixed cheesy grin, or make false attempts to look joyful whatever happens. However, I dare to believe that life is for living. It's not a sin to have fun or enjoy being a disciple of Jesus – in spite of the inevitable tough times we face. May I give you permission to smile occasionally?

Someone said, 'It takes seventeen muscles to smile and forty-three muscles to frown.'

BEING HOLY

In contrast to Christians taking themselves too seriously, we don't always take God's grace, love and power seriously enough. *Maybe Today* is an attempt to connect with those, like myself, who have faith and good intentions, but often feel like giving up the pursuit of holiness. Why? Because we think we can never be like the great women and men of faith we admire so much. We would like to emulate them, but instead of allowing them to inspire us, we find ourselves becoming disheartened. We somehow don't think Jesus can make us something we're not. What's more, we can be put off by strange ideas of what *holiness* is. Here's some good news: This book is less about *you* and more about what *God* can do in and through you, starting not with the big things in your life, but the little decisions you make day by day.

The apostle Paul prayed, 'May God himself, the God of peace, sanctify you through and through … The one who calls you is faithful and he will do it' (1 Thessalonians 5:23–24).

THANKS

I am indebted to those who have been a constant source of encouragement and practical help to me in my ministry, and especially in the writing of this book. A huge heartfelt thank you to the following:

- My ministerial colleagues at Methodist Central Hall, Westminster, for their fellowship, wisdom and good humour: Rev Martin Turner, Rev Dr Malcolm White, Rev Gordon Newton, Sister Jane Middleton and 'Boy Wonder', Pastor Jonathan Green.
- My initial proof readers: Ollie McEwen, Nadia Moreira, Kaye Lee and John Robins. Not forgetting my good-humoured editor, Sue, and all at CWR.
- My friends and colleagues who have graciously written words of commendation to persuade you to read, especially the lovely Diane for her Foreword.
- My friends at The Nationwide Christian Trust, especially Ray George and Canon Michael Cole, for allowing me to adapt a few thoughts that were originally written for past editions of *Living Light*.
- My colleagues at Premier Christian Radio and our regular listeners.
- Most importantly, my family: especially my brother-in-law and prayer partner, John Izzard; my children, Hannah and Jonathan, for their patience; and my soul mate and constant supporter, Frances. x

OMISSIONS

I'm a 'magpie' and collect anything bright and shiny. Except where original, or specifically acknowledged, other information included in this anthology is believed to be common knowledge or its origin unknown. The sources of this material are many and varied. Some illustrations, quotes and jokes have been noted after hearing people use them in conversations, sermons and other contexts – including emails, the internet and Christian publications (such as local church magazines). I am grateful for this material and any omissions of acknowledgement will be gladly corrected publicly on my blog (www.mayb2day.org.uk) and in future editions of this book. Where there is need for clarification, material I have written has the initials *TM*.

I pray that you will be inspired, challenged and uplifted by these reflections. Read on and enjoy!

Tony Miles

INTRODUCTION
WHAT IF? (PART I)

It was unfortunate that the wet paint sign had blown away

Warning: Each reflection in this book will only take a few minutes to read. But (and there's always a 'but') my introductions will take a little longer to peruse. Yes, I said 'introductions'. Some preachers seem to have lots of false endings to their sermons and never know when to stop! Well, you have the opposite here. If you can't be bothered to look at them, I'll forgive you. However, they will help you to understand the thinking behind the refrain that runs through these pages: 'Maybe today ...' I hope they will challenge you to allow Christ, by His Holy Spirit, to nurture holiness in your life.

Why is this book called Maybe Today?
I was watching the movie *Sliding Doors* starring Gwyneth Paltrow. Yes, I know it's peppered with bad language and has a few moments which might offend some, but I was challenged by the film's underlying message: in an instant, a person's life can be sent down one path instead of another. It raised for me the big 'What if?' question.

Sliding Doors is good value for money – two films in one! There are parallel storylines which commence as London publicist, Helen, dashes to catch a tube train. The movie explores what happens if a split second sends your life in two completely different directions. One story follows what happens after Helen fails to get on a tube train because a child blocks her way for a few seconds. The other depicts an entirely different chain of events. These come into play after Helen manages to enter the carriage having avoided the child and grasped the train's sliding door before it closes.

I commute into London regularly, so I can identify with just getting on or narrowly missing a tube train. I was only a few minutes behind one of the trains torn apart by the 7/7 bombings in 2005. Why? Well, simply because I was running late. I could easily have been in one of the devastated carriages and it's one of life's mysteries why I escaped. I can only begin to imagine with horror how different things could have been. I have tremendous sympathy for those caught up in it all.

All this left me thinking. You and I make split-second decisions every day about all sorts of things. What's more, they can make a far reaching difference to our lives and the lives of others. Let me give some examples of how momentary happenings can be regrettable:

- The man who loses his temper and strikes out at another.
- The teenager who decides to follow a bad influence.
- The couple in a passionate moment who have unprotected sex.
- The businessman who decides to leave out something significant on his tax return.
- The shopper who puts something in a bag without paying.

And so I could go on (and usually do). Some of these illustrations are extreme and could have been far more ordinary, but still significant.

Sliding Doors led me to thinking about my Christian faith. If split seconds can make such a difference, do I take them seriously? There are so many things I don't have power over, like bumping into a child when running for a train. Nevertheless, others are very much within my control, like deciding whether to say sorry to the child with whom I've had the collision, or whether to work late or come home early to see my family. It's easy to think that growing in holiness is about the big choices I make in life. The more I observe the lives of Christians who are shining examples, the more I'm convinced that the little decisions people make each day are equally important. Yet I often forget to pray about such things or sufficiently consider the implications of my hasty actions.

The late Rev Dr Rob Frost was known for the big and successful projects he'd launched and led, like the Share Jesus Missions, Easter People and countless other projects he took on tour nationally and internationally. He was an author and broadcaster, yet Rob was a good friend who cared, who released people's gifts, who encouraged, who prayed, who appreciated them, and who was there for them when they needed help or support.

Rob made positive decisions about the little things he considered important. Those who knew him well have valued and will remember these priorities. It's the Holy Spirit that helps us make the most of seemingly insignificant situations, so they become all-important. Hence, every opportunity is given for the light of Christ to shine through us – despite our faults. Often, God will work despite us and without our knowledge, but as we grow in faith we can make ourselves more available to be used by Him.

Questions:
- What will people say about you at your funeral?
- Are you happy with what you think people will say about you?
- When you meet Jesus face to face, what will He say about you?
- Are you concerned enough about that last question?

Now let us take a brief moment to remember God's love, grace and the forgiveness that's available through Christ … before we get too depressed by these questions! Paul said, 'for *all* have sinned and fall short of the glory of God …' (Romans 3:23, my italics). The good news is that, by trusting in what Jesus has done for us on the cross, we can know His forgiveness and help. This is a free gift, if only we'd receive it: 'For it is by grace you have been saved, through faith – and this is not from yourselves, it is the gift of God …' (Ephesians 2:8–9). I love Philip Yancey's book *What's So Amazing About Grace?* It's worth every penny. He writes, '*Grace means there is nothing we can do to make*

God love us more – no amount of spiritual calisthenics and reunifications, no amount of knowledge gained from seminaries and divinity schools, no amount of crusading on behalf of righteous causes. *And grace means there is nothing we can do to make God love us less* – no amount of racism or pride or pornography or adultery or even murder. Grace means that God already loves us as much as an infinite God can possibly love.'[1]

The trouble is, when I'm swept along by the pace of today's world, I doubt I'll ever become the man of God I should be. In his book *Get A Life*, Paul Valler writes, 'We may have a sense of what God is calling us to do, but be trapped by a self-image that is a barrier in the mind. That limiting self-image can be age, family background, past failures or comments people have made in the past (such as "You're no good", or "You'll never achieve anything"). God seems to specialize in using people who feel weak. "God chose the weak things of the world to shame the strong" (1 Corinthians 1:27).'[2] Well, that's encouraging!

Nevertheless, when I'm busy and stressed, how can I make good decisions – when I'm full of a cocktail of goodness and evil? Paul captures something of this struggle: 'For what I do is not the good I want to do ... For what I want to do I do not do, but what I hate I do' (Romans 7:19,15b). Some preachers are very good at telling us how we should behave as Christians, but they never help us unlock the power to do those things. They exhort us to try harder in our discipleship, but they don't tell us the all-important and essential factor. It's as though it's some sort of a secret! Stay tuned and I'll share the secret in Intro. Part 2. It's up next!

GETTING CAUGHT UP IN THE LIFE OF GOD (PART 2)

Are you ready for the secret? This is how we change our lives and become more like Jesus: Major W. Ian Thomas, the founder of Torchbearers – an international evangelistic organisation –

wrote about the mystery of godliness. He said, 'The moment you come to realise that only God can make a man godly, you are left with no option but to find God, and to know God, and to let God be God in and through you, whoever He may be and this will leave you with no margin for picking and choosing for there is only one God, and He is absolute, and He made you expressly for Himself!'[3]

I passionately believe the secret to holiness is learning what it means to be 'in Christ' and for 'Christ to be in us'. Paul writes, 'I have been crucified with Christ and I no longer live, but *Christ lives in me*. The life I live in the body, I live by faith in the Son of God, who loved me and gave himself for me' (Galatians 2:20, my italics).

You and I only 'fight the good fight' and win the battle over apathy and temptation in our lives when we allow Jesus to work within us. He then guides us towards making positive and considered decisions in the face of everyday challenges.

The secret is inviting God to reside within us and to get caught up in a relationship with the Divine. This has been likened by some to a dance (*perichoresis* – Greek word for dance and a metaphor for the Trinity). Eugene H. Peterson, writer of *The Message*, wrote the following:

> Imagine a folk dance, a round dance, with three partners in each set. The music starts up and the partners holding hands begin moving in a circle. On signal from the caller, they release hands, change partners, and weave in and out, swinging first one and then another. The tempo increases, the partners move more swiftly with and between and among one another, swinging and twirling, embracing and releasing, holding on and letting go. But there is no confusion, every movement is cleanly coordinated in precise rhythms (these are practiced and skillful dancers!), as each person maintains his or her own identity. To the onlooker, the movements are so swift it is impossible at times to distinguish one person

from another; the steps are so intricate that it is difficult
to anticipate the actual configurations as they appear:
Perichoresis (*peri* = around; *choresis* = dance).[4]

In order to prepare ourselves for the dance of God, it helps to:
- worship regularly.
- ensure that we pray about all things, however briefly.
- stop limiting prayer to particular circumstances, times and places.
- be in fellowship with other Christians, including those different
  from us, or with whom we disagree.
- feed ourselves spiritually – especially on God's Word.

These things help to develop a relationship for dancing, which
can set us free to be who we are to be in Jesus.

'Christ in us' may be the key, but it still isn't easy when we're
up against it! It's hard to make time to nurture a relationship in
a pressurised digital society, when time's at a premium:

> We are constantly texting or talking on our mobiles, or keeping in
> touch with friends and strangers
> whether it be MSN, or social networks, like Facebook.
> Yet, we have no time for our Creator.
> We fire off emails here, there and everywhere, with little thought,
> and we do the same with our prayers and our reading.
> We find there's little time to listen, which isn't surprising for,
> as soon as there's any silence, we put on our iPods, radios, or TVs.
> We know more about the global village we live in
> and what everyone thinks, but we're frightened to find out too
> much about ourselves
> and the difference we can make to the world.
> We let our lives be taken over by uncontrolled 'To Do Lists'
> which are dictated by others, or even by our own need to be
> wanted and valued.
> We work long hours to earn more to pay the rent or a mortgage
> for a property we're rarely able to relax in,
> because we are too busy working to pay for the roof over our heads.

We spend a lot of our cash on so called 'labour saving' devices,
but we don't seem to have any more time.
We travel more than ever in cars, buses,
trains, aircraft and boats,
because we are able to do so.
Yet, we don't think a lot about
our spiritual journey through life;
we're always doing, but never being;
we are missing
the
point
!

The next time you're reading the Gospel according to John, notice that he presents us with plenty of contrasts and choices: light/darkness, truth/falsehood, life/death, sight/blindness, good/evil, shepherd/wolf, love/hate, day/night, faith/doubt and so on.

Maybe today is the day to start choosing! But before we do anything, remember again it starts with Jesus, who said, 'You did not choose me, but I chose you and appointed you to go and bear fruit – fruit that will last. Then the Father will give you whatever you ask in my name. This is my command: Love each other' (John 15:16–17). Once we know that we've been chosen by His grace, we then live in love guided by the Spirit of Christ who helps us to choose wisely: 'This day I call heaven and earth as witnesses against you that I have set before you life and death, blessings and curses. Now choose life, so that you and your children may live …' (Deuteronomy 30:19).

But, what is holiness?
The only way for us to grow in holiness is to surrender ourselves more and more to God through Jesus. We long to please Him and He inspires us to travel the right way, rather than presenting us with rules we must follow. His heart becomes our heart.

Saviour from sin, I wait to prove
That Jesus is thy healing name;
To lose, when perfected in love,
Whate'er I have, or can, or am.
I stay me on thy faithful word:
The servant shall be as his Lord.

Answer that gracious end in me
For which thy precious life was given;
Redeem from all iniquity,
Restore, and make me meet for heaven:
Unless thou purge my every stain,
Thy suffering and my faith are vain.

Didst thou not die that I might live
No longer to myself, but thee,
Might body, soul, and spirit give
To him who gave himself for me?
Come then, my Master and my God,
Take the dear purchase of thy blood.

Thine own devoted servant claim
For thine own truth and mercy's sake;
Hallow in me thy glorious name;
Me for thine own this moment take,
And change, and throughly purify;
Thine only may I live and die.

*Charles Wesley – hymn-writer, poet, evangelist and co-founder of the Methodist
movement with his brother, John (1707–1788)*

SMILE

'Holiness consists of doing the will of God with a smile.'

*Mother Teresa of Calcutta – Albanian Roman Catholic nun (1910–1997) as quoted
by Billy Graham in* The Secret of Happiness

PRAYER

Lord Jesus, my Saviour and Friend,
may Your Holy Spirit permeate every part of my being.
Cleanse and heal me, revive and renew me,
Equip and enable me, strengthen and empower me,
that I may live for You and be set apart for You.
May my words and actions bear witness to Your love
and may I be set free to obtain life in all its fullness,
with the hope of eternal glory in my heart,
for Your kingdom's sake. Amen.

THERE'S ORDER IN 'RANDOM' (PART 3)

This is the last bit of my introduction – honest! It only needs
to be read if you're likely to be puzzled by such an *ad hoc*
collection of thoughts.

'Dad, you're so *random*!' My teenage children, Hannah and
Jonathan, are never backward in coming forward, especially
when it comes to telling their dad what they think of him. I
suppose sometimes my observations, quips and humour can be
arbitrary and unpredictable. Hannah and Jonathan just think
I'm 'mad', 'crazy', or 'bonkers' – and sometimes all three. But,
they would. Little do they know that they have *random* moments
too – perhaps that's one of the reasons I love them so much! I
guess as we grow to understand each other more, we'll realise
that we're not quite so *random* after all. There are patterns to our
behaviour and often reasons for the way we behave which reflect
our characters, past experiences, knowledge and other influences.

Why do I mention this? Okay it is pretty *random* in itself, but I
guess it's because I've come to appreciate that the God I worship
is often mysterious and not as predictable as people would like
to think. The kingdom of God is often more messy than I, by
nature, feel comfortable with. As a methodical Methodist, I
like things to be planned, ordered and consistent. Yet, it's what
I call 'divine randomness' that stops me being complacent and

keeps me on my spiritual toes. Now, don't get me wrong, I'm sure that God is dependable and reliable in His nature and there are good reasons for His mysterious and surprising behaviour. Nevertheless, I have to accept that there are some things, such as healing, I'll never fully understand this side of heaven.

Let me simply point out that whilst Christians believe that their Creator brings order out of chaos and is consistent in love, people will never completely fathom the depth of His being or the extent of His grace this side of Glory. His Holy Spirit is likened to a wind that blows where it pleases (John 3:8). I'm praying that the wind of the Holy Spirit will use this random collection of thoughts in this book and apply them appropriately to your heart.

The Pharisees were passionately devout, yet their confident, systematic (albeit selective) theology missed out on what God was doing by the Holy Spirit. Why? Because Jesus' ministry must have appeared *random* and radical. In short, our Maker and Sustainer may not be as *random* as we tend to think at first. The deeper our relationship with the Trinity, the more we should glimpse God's nature, trust His will, be open to surprises, and make way for a bit of disorder in our lives. Thankfully, God is ever-patient, understands us completely and believes in us.

In a nutshell, I want you to see each day as an opportunity to ponder the *'Maybe today'* question. Let God help you to choose wisely and to make decisions that can enable you to grow in holiness and be an effective Christian witness. It's about learning to listen and be reflective – even when you're in a hurry; it's about asking the right questions and allowing Christ within to prompt you, rather than spending hours agonising over what's right or wrong; it's about pondering *'what if?'* rather than regretfully finding yourself tormented by *'if only'* after you've paid insufficient attention to the decisions you make.

Maybe today, we need to learn to be open to surprises, spontaneous in love and ready to be caught up in the dance of God's kingdom!

JUST LISTEN

A meditation to be read without any hurry and reflectively.
Why not find somewhere that is quiet and be alone as you let the
words speak? Perhaps you can go for a walk, or sit in a garden –
anywhere, but try to avoid interruptions. Take your time.

Ssssshhh.
Be quiet.
Yes … you!
Hush and listen.
No! … I mean really listen,
carefully and prayerfully.
Stop what you are doing and thinking right now.
Be still
and learn to listen properly.
Just listen!

Put aside your 'To Do' list and your agenda.
Put aside your guilt and your frustration.
Put aside your plans, hopes and dreams;
and simply be!
Rest your thoughts,
relieve your mind
and calm your restless soul.
Just listen!

Listen to your heart
and relax to the rhythm of your body
– a temple of the Holy Spirit.
Let the strong arms of your Creator embrace you
– the One who gave you the very breath of life.
Allow the sounds of God's creation to be a lullaby
that rocks you in the cradle of divine love
and know that you are enfolded in the duvet of His peace;
that deep peace that passes all human understanding.
Just listen!

Find that place deep within you
and be still and know that God is with you by the gift of His
Spirit.
Remember that He loves you far more than you could ever
imagine.
You are cherished,
despite your failings,
despite your faithlessness,
despite your inability to take control of your life,
or even to influence the lives of others.
Hear the still small voice of acceptance.
Wait for it.
Just listen!

You are chosen.
You are needed.
You are understood ... completely!
You can be forgiven and renewed.
Bask for a moment in grace and mercy.
Go on ... enjoy it!
For life is a gift.
Find out in the stillness who you really are
and what is important
– most important!
Just listen!

Allow the balm of God's healing to soothe you.
Oh yes ... and understand this:
Unless you listen more often,
I mean, really listen;
unless you open the floodgates of your heart to God's Spirit,
you will never find the inrush of life in all its fullness,
you will never find true meaning and purpose.
Rather, you will find yourself dancing to the wrong tune,
or pounding a pointless treadmill.
You will find that you will grow tired and weary,

you will stumble and fall,
you will never soar with those wings clipped!
Just listen!

So, do yourself a favour
and listen, precious one;
listen with care and attention;
listen and live.
For you are loved unconditionally by your Maker
– the One who sent His Son
to set you free;
free to soar on wings like eagles.
He longs for you to trust,
respond
and receive all that He has for you.
BUT, for heaven's sake
… just listen!

TM

THE PACE OF LIFE

01 SLOW DOWN – YOU MOVE TOO FAST!

On my way to work I was crossing an iron bridge in order to get to the London-bound platform. I had only just started up the steps when a tube train pulled into the station. My brisk pace became a run so I could get on the train. Unfortunately, my legs were moving quicker than my brain at that time of the morning and I missed one of the first downward steps and quite spectacularly fell down to the bottom. I survived with cuts, grazes, some aches and pains, and a bruised pride. How embarrassing!

I did get on the train, but as I was brushing myself down, I had to ask myself, 'Why was I rushing?' The fact is, I don't know. I wasn't late and no one would have minded if I had arrived at my destination ten minutes later. The dash certainly wasn't worth a potential broken leg.

MAYBE TODAY is a day for asking, 'Who is dictating the pace of my life?' Do you find that your life always seems to be set against the clock and the speed of life is constantly escalating, despite all the labour-saving and time-saving devices you have available to you? If so, hear the word that God whispered in my ear as I nursed my wounds, 'Slow down, you fool … Be still, and know that I am God'.

PRAYER

Lord Jesus, help me to resist the rat race, and to be a non-conformist who walks purposefully to my destination, guided by Your Spirit and held in Your love. Amen.

BIBLE READING

BE STILL **Psalm 46**

I DO NOT GIVE TO YOU AS THE WORLD GIVES **John 14:23–27**

FURTHER REFLECTION

Creator God, You are the giver of life.
As I embark on another day's journey with You,
be with me in my chores and responsibilities;
in my working and playing;
in my activity and resting;
in my sighing and laughing;
in my speaking and listening;
in my reading and writing;
in my thinking and praying.
I dedicate this day to You,
asking You to forgive, heal and equip me,
that I may be ready for today's challenges and opportunities.
In all things may Your Spirit of grace and humility
guide and direct me in the ways of peace and joy.
So, loving God, may this day be lived for You,
for those I love, and those I ought to love,
for the sake of Jesus, my Saviour, example and friend. Amen.

TM

SMILE

The early bird may get the worm,
but it's the second mouse that gets the cheese.

Anon.

02 LIFE'S TOO SHORT

My car was passed by an articulated lorry which was obviously in a hurry. It was delivering food for a well-known frozen food chain. The slogan on the side of the container caught my eye: 'Because life's too short to peel carrots'. Personally, I prefer fresh vegetables to those that are frozen or processed. Yet, supermarkets are keen to meet the demand for food that can be prepared in minutes.

I found myself mentally pausing on the frantic M25. I asked myself, 'Why do we so readily swallow the myth that life's too short to peel carrots?' Who says so? What do we do with all the time that so called 'labour saving devices' or 'convenience products' afford us? Somehow we don't *save* time at all. In fact, life seems *more* pressured. People in their eighties or nineties appear to have had more time in the 'old days', when carrots had to be peeled and they didn't have motorways!

MAYBE TODAY you could take time to do something that many consider *life's too short* to do. We work longer, travel more and continually feel we have to be more productive. Consider it a radical action to go against the flow and slow down. The story attributed to Aesop about the tortoise and the hare comes to mind. It's ironic that the high-tech solution to M25 traffic jams is the introduction of variable speed controls. We've discovered that you can go faster if you actually slow down!

PRAYER

Lord of Eternity, help me to discern what I need to take more time over today. Amen.

BIBLE READING

JESUS HAS A LOT TO DO **Luke 4:38–44**
COMMIT YOUR WAY TO THE LORD **Psalm 37:1–9**

FURTHER REFLECTION

Lord, temper with tranquillity
our manifold activity,
that we may do our work for Thee
with very great simplicity.

Attributed to a sixteenth-century monk

'Men of lofty genius when they are doing the least work are the
most active'

*Leonardo da Vinci – Italian artist, scientist, designer, engineer and genius
(1452–1519)*

SMILE

Someone once said, 'It's not the pace of life that concerns me,
it's the sudden stop at the end.'

Anon.

03 OVERLOAD

What's your week been like? Quiet or full? I find myself
increasingly exhausted and overloaded in this fast-moving
generation. It was Henry Kissinger, the former American
Secretary of State, who once said, 'Next week there can't be any
crisis – my schedule is already full.' I can sympathise with him!
If I'm not careful my diary can have a life of its own; it can take
control of my life, rather than serving it. It's then that I find
myself justifying relaxation, reflection or family time. I don't
think this is what God wants my life to be like. Sometimes the
pressure comes from others, such as an employer, but I must
also take some responsibility and think about my priorities.
Management books often quote a Captain J.A. Hatfield who
said, 'The art of resting the mind and the power of dismissing
from it all care and worry is probably one of the secrets of our
great men.' And women, of course!

MAYBE TODAY is a day for taming your diary, resting your
mind, and thinking about your quality of life. For if your days
become too full, you may well find yourself heading for an
unscheduled and unwelcome crisis! David Allen in his excellent
book *Getting Things Done* writes, 'What you *do* with your time,
what you *do* with information, and what you *do* with your body
and your focus relative to your priorities – those are the real
options to which you must allocate your limited resources. The
real issue is how to make appropriate choices about what to *do*
at any point in time. The real issue is how we manage *actions*.'[1]

PRAYER

*God of life and peace, help me to take time to smell the roses and
to use Your gift of time wisely. Amen.*

BIBLE READING

REST FOR THE WEARY **Matthew 11:25–30**
PREPARE YOUR MINDS FOR ACTION **1 Peter 1:13–16**

FURTHER REFLECTION

The clock is my dictator, I shall not rest.
It makes me lie down only when exhausted.
It leads me into deep depression, it hounds my soul.
It leads me in circles of frenzy for activities' sake.
Even though I run frantically from task to task,
I will never get it all done, for my "ideal" is with me.
Deadlines and my need for approval, they drive me.
They demand performance from me, beyond the limits of my schedule.
They anoint my head with migraines, my in-basket over-flows.
Surely fatigue and time pressure shall follow me all the days of my life,
And I will dwell in the bonds of frustration forever.

Marcia K. Hornok, Psalm 23, Antithesis [2]

SMILE

'Work is the refuge of people who have nothing better to do.'
Oscar Wilde – witty Irish playwright, poet and author (1854–1900)

'If we keep doing what we're doing, we're going to keep getting what we're getting.'
Dr Stephen R. Covey – Leadership authority, an organisational consultant, teacher and author (1932–)

04 SLEEP

I am often riding on the London Underground at an early hour of the morning. It amused me on one occasion to observe that out of the twelve people sitting near me, only four were awake. Two of us were smiling at the one who was snoring loudly, and at another almost resting on the shoulder of the person sitting next to him. I have been conscious ever since then that I might behave in a similar fashion when I doze off!

How sleepy are you today? Well, apparently many of us are 'sleep deprived'. Our high-paced lifestyle is causing us to get insufficient sleep. Moreover, sleep disorders like snoring and insomnia are not helping, if they aren't symptoms themselves. Most people are unaware of their desperate need of more rest and GPs don't always diagnose the problem.

All this raises the question: Do we take sleep seriously? I'm not talking about during sermons – like Eutychus in Acts 20:9. I mean planned sleep – part of our re-creation. The Bible says that God rested on the seventh day after His creative activity. We call the seventh day the 'Sabbath' – from the Hebrew word meaning 'to rest', both physically and mentally. I think there should be a 'Sabbath' in every day. We all need different amounts of sleep to function effectively. So we need to find the amount of rest that is adequate for us.

MAYBE TODAY is a day for planning rest into your schedule and for allowing yourself appropriate time to sleep and dream, without feeling guilty. Jesus said, 'Come to me all you who are weary and burdened, and I will give you rest' (Matthew 11:28).

PRAYER

For sleeping and dreaming in the land of Nod, we praise You, re-creating God. Amen.

BIBLE READING

OUR CREATOR SETS AN EXAMPLE **Genesis 2:1–3**
EUTYCHUS – SLEEP DEPRIVED? **Acts 20:7–12**

FURTHER REFLECTION

Now that the sun has set,
I sit and rest, and think of you.
Give my weary body peace.
Let my legs and arms stop aching,
Let my nose stop sneezing,
Let my head stop thinking.
Let me sleep in your arms.

African Dinka Prayer

SMILE

'Many churches are now serving coffee after the sermon.
Presumably this is to get the people thoroughly awake
before they start to drive home.'

Anon.

'If you want your dreams to come true, don't oversleep.'

Anon.

05 PEACE

I remember hearing the story of three artists who were each asked to paint a picture that summed up the word 'peace' for them. One captured the sight of a beautiful sunset. The second saw 'peace' in a lake with some snow-capped mountains in the background – the scene depicted the majesty of the mountain range mirrored in the perfectly still water. Wonderful.

The third artist, however, saw 'peace' differently, portraying a raging white water river with action and spray everywhere. When questioned where the peace was in the scene, he pointed out a little bird in the foreground that was resting, perched on a rock with all the commotion taking place around it. 'This,' he said, 'is peace. This bird found its place of rest and stillness in the midst of it all.'

I find this honest and helpful. J. Oswald Sanders once said, 'Peace is not the absence of trouble, but the presence of God.'

MAYBE TODAY is a day for finding your rock in the midst of life's activity and challenges. We have never been promised an easy life, only an inner harmony in the midst of it all. Remember that Jesus, our rock, was present with His disciples in the storm and enabled them to find peace and stillness.

PRAYER

Let us pray with the psalmist, 'I will lie down and sleep in peace, for you alone, O LORD, make me dwell in safety' (Psa. 4:8). Amen.

BIBLE READING

PERFECT PEACE FOR THOSE WHO TRUST **Isaiah 26**
HE SET MY FEET ON A ROCK **Psalm 40**

FURTHER REFLECTION

Drop thy still dews of quietness,
Till all our strivings cease;
Take from our souls the strain and stress,
And let our ordered lives confess
The beauty of thy peace.

John Greenleaf Whittier – American Quaker poet and abolitionist (1807–1892)

SMILE

'Daddy, why do you always say,
"*a piece* of the Lord be with you?"'

Hannah Miles – my daughter (aged 4)

06 WAITING

'Lord give me patience, but give it to me now!' Have you ever prayed like that? I have. When stuck in traffic on the M25, for example; or when my train is halted because of signal failure; or when in a static queue at a bank or surgery and the ticket for the car park is about to expire. Like it or not, life is full of 'times of waiting'!

There's plenty of waiting in the Bible, from Israel's wanderings in the wilderness, to the disciples being told to wait in Jerusalem for the gift of the Holy Spirit. Somehow God uses 'times of waiting', and often requires them to further His purposes.

I always think the Saturday of Holy Week is a strange 'waiting day'. It's the time between Good Friday and Easter Day – a day of mixed emotions. Looking backwards, there's grief and despair at remembering Jesus' death; looking forwards, there's anticipation and hope with Easter just around the corner.

MAYBE TODAY is a day for offering to God 'times of waiting', whilst being honest about any feelings of frustration – especially when things appear empty and hopeless!

PRAYER

Lord, use my waiting today and may Your Holy Spirit enable me to die to selfishness and impatience, and rise to the place of Your will for me. Amen.

BIBLE READING

THE WAITING DAY **Matthew 27:62–66**
JESUS' INSTRUCTIONS TO WAIT **Acts 1:4–11**

FURTHER REFLECTION

O blessed Jesus, give me stillness of soul in Thee.
Let Thy mighty calmness reign in me;
Rule me, O King of gentleness, King of peace.
Give me control, great power of self-control,
Control over my words, thoughts and actions.
From all irritability, want of meekness, want of gentleness,
dear Lord, deliver me.
By Thine own deep patience, give me patience.
Make me in this and all things more and more like Thee.

*St John of the Cross – Spanish Christian mystic, poet, and Carmelite monk
(1542–1591)*

SMILE

During a particularly long service a small voice was heard
asking: 'Mummy, is it still Sunday?'

Anon.

07 TEXTS AND PRAYERS

I'm pretty hopeless when it comes to sending text messages; despite the fact that I have now mastered predictive texting. By the time I've typed out what I want to say, I could have rung the person concerned … and three other people too! Text language is also a mystery to me. For a long time I thought that *LOL* at the end of a message meant *Lots of love*, until I discovered it meant *Laugh out loud*. I did think some people were being surprisingly intimate.

Texting and other modern forms of communication are good ways of keeping in touch. In fact, my children will sometimes tell me more in a text, or via *MSN*, than over the dinner table. However, I do worry a little that it may affect the way people correspond more generally. Will people lose the art of writing more considered letters or emails to each other? Will all interaction gradually become shorter and more superficial? And what about the way we communicate with God? Do we abbreviate and hurry our prayers?

MAYBE TODAY could be a day for expressing something that should be articulated properly and leisurely – even to tell someone you love them in more than a few syllables. Perhaps that 'someone' could be the God who's taken time to communicate with you and who longs for a considered reply.

PRAYER

hi God! Soz 4 my qik msgs. help me 2 cool it in da future. Nevertheless, most merciful Creator, when my humble intercessions and supplications abound with prolific nonsensical words that convey not the reality of my experience, may Your forgiveness also be known in the inner depths of my being. Then, help me to get real and strike the right balance! Amen.

BIBLE READING

PAUL WRITES AND PRAYS **Ephesians 3:14–21**
JESUS TEACHES ABOUT PRAYER **Matthew 6:5–15**

FURTHER REFLECTION

'Where your prayer is, there your heart is.'
Anon.

'A man who prays much in private will make short prayers in public.'
Dwight L. Moody – North American evangelist (1837–1899)

SMILE

Two young boys were spending the night at their grandparents' home. At bedtime, the two boys knelt beside their beds to say their prayers when the youngest one began praying at the top of his voice. 'I pray for a Nintendo Wii … I pray for an iPod … I pray for a new mobile phone.' His older brother leaned over and nudged the younger brother and said, 'Why are you shouting your prayers? God isn't deaf.' To which the little brother replied quietly, 'No, but Grandma is!'

Anon.

REST MY WEARY SOUL

When time is short and my 'To Do' list is long,
O Lord, rest my weary soul.
When the deadlines loom and my work is not finished,
O Lord, rest my weary soul.
When the technology is wonderful but sometimes lets
me down,
O Lord, rest my weary soul.
When technology is reliable but I make mistakes,
O Lord, rest my weary soul.
When the objective is clear but the ethical issues are
cloudy,
O Lord, rest my weary soul.
When those in authority give me instructions that
challenge my integrity,
O Lord, rest my weary soul.
When political correctness is rife and Christian witness
is hard,
O Lord, rest my weary soul.
When my church cares but fails to understand the
broadcast industry,
O Lord, rest my weary soul.
When my work keeps me from my family and leisure,
O Lord, rest my weary soul.
Hear my prayer for peace, renewal, and restoration.
Loving Lord, You said,
'Come to me all who are weary and heavy laden and I
will give you rest.'
Help me to respond to Your invitation and receive Your
promise.
Then, may I trust You in the week ahead,
and know Your life-giving Holy Spirit sustaining me
in the place You would have me be,
for Your love's sake. Amen.
TM

REACHING OUT

08 HEY THERE, LONELY GIRL!

I saw a commuter crying the other side of a jam-packed carriage on the underground. The woman was obviously deeply upset. She held her head in her hands and tears washed mascara down her cheeks. I found it strange that few people noticed and that nobody left their comfort zone to comfort her. Why? Was it for fear of interfering, or being misunderstood? In that moment I had an overwhelming sense of God's love for her.

MAYBE TODAY is a day for being conscious of the heartbroken and lonely, even in the midst of the crowds and the laughter. Jesus had time for people and noticed their need. Be sure to open your eyes and your heart wherever your journey takes you today.

PRAYER

Loving God, by Your Spirit, comfort the sorrowful and accompany the lonely – even through me. In Jesus' name, I pray. Amen.

BIBLE READING

HE CARES FOR YOU **1 Peter 5:6–11**
DO NOT BE AFRAID **Deuteronomy 31:1–8**

FURTHER REFLECTION

When I feel abandoned and alone,
help me to cry out to You in all honesty.
Assure me of Your loving presence,
and may Your everlasting arms embrace and comfort me.
In Jesus' name, I pray. Amen.
TM

SMILE

'When it rains, is it God's tears?'[1]

Hannah Miles – my daughter (aged 7)

'I never will understand all the good that a simple smile can accomplish.'

Mother Teresa of Calcutta – Albanian Roman Catholic nun (1910–1997)

09 REJOICING AND WEEPING

Teenagers were shrieking with joy, hugging, and smiling broadly. They had just received their GCSE results and it was good to see that many of the young people were pleased with their news. However, as I observed from a distance, I could see the disappointment, pain and worry on the faces of a few quiet students who were making their way through the rowdy throng towards their anxious parents. Brokenness and tears were present in the midst of the rejoicing – unnoticed by the otherwise preoccupied majority. Just a few had the sensitivity to engage in conversation with their crestfallen friends and to put a consoling arm around them.

From my vantage point the emotional contrasts were clear to see. Yet, needs of others were less obvious, and easily overlooked, by those in the middle of the crowd and caught up in all the excitement.

MAYBE TODAY you could pray that the Holy Spirit will enable you to grow in sensitivity and have an intuition that notices individual needs that others frequently miss. Laughter and tears are often not far from each other. Paul urges us to 'Rejoice with those who rejoice; mourn with those who mourn' (Romans 12:15). Remember, too, that someone said, 'Your worst days are never so bad that you're beyond the reach of God's grace. And your best days are never so good that you're beyond the need of God's grace.'

PRAYER

Forgive me, Lord, when I am so full of myself that I fail to share the joys or sorrows of my neighbours. Amen.

BIBLE READING

Love **Romans 12:9–21**
Joy and sorrow near Jerusalem **Luke 19:37–44**

FURTHER REFLECTION

God of infinite love, we know You to be Father, Son and Holy Spirit,
one God but in a community of relationship and expression.
You are watching over this troubled city;
weeping over this city; aching for this city;
and enfolding this city with Your everlasting arms.
Protect and keep us, feed and teach us;
nurture and inspire us; guide and enable us.
Help us to make a worthwhile contribution to community life
and all our relationships, that society may know peace with justice,
love with respect; healing with joy; and hope for a brighter tomorrow,
through Jesus Christ our Lord and Saviour. Amen.
TM

SMILE
'Happiness is having a large, loving, caring, close-knit family ... in another city.'
George Burns – American comedian, actor and writer (1896–1996)

10 THE PIETÀ

For a special birthday present, my wife Frances treated me to
a few days away to Italy's capital. You could say it was a *rome...*
antic weekend! It was a whistle-stop tour, but we managed to
include a visit to the Vatican. A highlight for us was being able
to see a sculpture by the 21-year-old Michelangelo: the Pietà. It's
carved out of a single block of Carrara marble and can be found
on the right-hand side as you enter St. Peter's Church.

In perfect life-size proportions, it depicts Mary holding her
son, Jesus. Mary looks very serene, but unlike most pictures
of her cradling her newborn baby son, Michelangelo has her
embracing her crucified son. It is an ostensibly hopeless scene.
Yet, if you look at Mary's two hands, Michelangelo depicts love
and grief, alongside resolution and surrender. For although
Mary's left hand is embracing her son's lifeless body, the other
is clearly held open towards God, in acceptance and faithful
submission to His will.

MAYBE TODAY you could find inspiration in the Pietà,
especially if you are remembering in your prayers those who
are hurting and grieving. Maybe you can reach out to embrace
people with love and comfort on the one hand, whilst raising the
other in intercession for them, in openness to the Holy Spirit,
and in hope as you surrender their situation to God's will? If you
are grieving yourself, why not reflect on Michelangelo's message
in the marble and allow it to speak to you.

PRAYER

*Loving God, may I know Your everlasting arms cradling me today
and pointing me to the risen Jesus – my comfort, my hope, my
Saviour. Amen.*

BIBLE READING

THE RESURRECTION BODY **1 Corinthians 15:35–57**
MARY'S SONG **Luke 1:46–55**

FURTHER REFLECTION

'We give them back to you, O God, those whom you gave to us.
You did not lose them when you gave them to us, and we do not
lose them by their return to you. Your Son has taught us that
life is eternal and love cannot die. So death is only a horizon,
and a horizon is only the limit of our sight. Open our eyes to see
more clearly, and draw us closer to you, so that we may know
we are nearer to our loved ones, who are with you. You have
told us that you are preparing a place for us: prepare us, that
where you are we may be always, O dear Lord of life and death.'

*William Penn – English Quaker and the founder of the colony of Pennsylvania
(1644–1718)*

SMILE
'It's hard to understand how cemeteries can raise their
burial charges and blame the cost of living.'

Anon.

11 BEING PREPARED TO FORGIVE

I was returning from an Ash Wednesday service. Exhausted, I flopped into my car and switched on the radio to relax. I was puzzled because I couldn't get a reception for any radio station. It then occurred to me that someone had stolen my aerial. Why do little things bug me so much? Was it the inconvenience, the inevitable replacement cost, or the cheek of the thief that riled me? Whatever, I wasn't a happy bunny and didn't feel very forgiving. C.S. Lewis said, 'Everyone says forgiveness is a lovely idea, until they have something to forgive.'

I then remembered that *repentance and forgiveness* had been our focus in church. What a short memory I have! I expect God to forgive me, but I fail to treat others likewise. Admittedly, the thief hadn't shown any repentance or asked for forgiveness. Yet, if I'm honest, my feelings were more than righteous indignation; they didn't come from a forgiving heart.

MAYBE TODAY you could reflect on whether you are prepared to forgive as you have been forgiven. You may not have been asked for forgiveness, but is your heart prepared? We read in Matthew 18:21 that Peter asked Jesus, "'Lord, how many times shall I forgive my brother when he sins against me? Up to seven times?" Jesus answered, "I tell you, not seven times, but seventy-seven times."' In some translations it says 'seventy times seven'. It's a simple formula: 70 x 7 = God's love. The art is learning the formula and owning it before you need it!

PRAYER

Merciful Lord, teach me that true forgiveness is being ready to embrace the one who has hurt me before I need to do so. Amen.

BIBLE READING

THE PARABLE OF THE UNMERCIFUL SERVANT
Matthew 18:21–35
JUDGING OTHERS **Luke 6:37–42**

FURTHER REFLECTION

'To err is human, to forgive, divine.'

Alexander Pope – English poet (1688–1744)

SMILE

'Always forgive your enemies – nothing annoys them so much.'

Oscar Wilde – witty Irish playwright, poet and author (1854–1900)

'Hey, minister! I've just seen someone stealing your car from the church car park. Don't worry though, I managed to get the number before they drove off.'

Anon.

12 HOSPITALITY

When I was training at theological college, one of my friends lived in student accommodation with his family. I'll never forget the mat that lay outside his front door. On it were printed these words, 'Oh no, not you again!' It always made me smile. I don't think he only put it out when he knew I was calling! Though, let's be honest, I'm sure we all know people who are hard to welcome and for whom such a mat might be highly appropriate.

Nevertheless, Paul says Christians should 'practise hospitality' (Romans 12:13). In other words, hospitality should be a Christian characteristic. It's surprising how often issues relating to hospitality are mentioned in the Bible. Jesus, for example, said, 'But when you give a banquet, invite the poor, the crippled, the lame, the blind, and you will be blessed. Although they cannot repay you, you will be repaid at the resurrection of the righteous' (Luke 14:13–14).

I'm very conscious that it can be psychologically difficult for many people to enter a church building – especially if it's not their custom. Hence it's so important for those of us who are Christians to demonstrate our concern for people who live near us and show that we are interested in them. It is part of our witness.

MAYBE TODAY is a day for loving someone who is hard to love, or welcoming someone you are usually tempted to turn away: 'Do not forget to entertain strangers, for by so doing some people have entertained angels without knowing it' (Hebrews 13:2).

PRAYER

Lord, help me to see people as You see them and embrace them with Your love. Amen.

BIBLE READING

LOVE EACH OTHER DEEPLY **1 Peter 4:7–11**
JESUS AT A PHARISEE'S HOUSE **Luke 14:1–14**

FURTHER REFLECTION

'To give our Lord a perfect hospitality, Mary and Martha must combine.' (See Luke 10:38–42)

St Teresa of Avila – Spanish Carmelite nun (1515-1582)

SMILE

The Bishop was the dinner guest. The table beautifully prepared and the food looked delicious. They were ready to begin. The hostess spoke to her daughter, aged six. 'Mary, you say Grace, please.' A rather long delay ensued. The mother coaxed the little girl, 'Come on, Mary, say what you heard me say this morning at breakfast.' In a loud voice it came out, 'O God, why did I invite the Bishop to dinner tonight?'[2]

Anon.

13 KNOWN BY NAME

Global Vision was once the theme at the Christian event Easter People. Speakers were drawn from across the world, one of whom spoke of India's 18 million street children. He told of a homeless little girl who stroked a colleague's arm and, rather than asking for sweets, money or food, simply looked up at the woman longingly with a simple request: 'Please, just say my name.'

Names are terribly important. Nobody is merely a number, statistic or 'a case'. Our names are chosen for us, either before we are born, or soon afterwards. So, whether we're called John Smith, or Engelbert Humperdinck, our Creator knows us intimately and loves us perfectly: God said, 'Fear not, for I have redeemed you; I have summoned you by name; you are mine' (Isa. 43:1b).

When Mary Magdalene was crying outside the tomb, the risen Jesus stood before her and said, 'Mary' (John 20:16). Despite the darkness and her despair, the Lord spoke her name and immediately she knew she'd seen the Lord.

MAYBE TODAY is a day for ensuring you speak to people by name, so that they know they matter and are loved. By simply using someone's name, it may be that they will see the risen Lord in you.

PRAYER

Lord Jesus, I thank You that I am known and loved. May all who are at their wits' end today, hear You speaking their name tenderly. Amen.

BIBLE READING

JESUS APPEARS TO MARY MAGDALENE **John 20:10–18**
SHEEP CALLED BY NAME **John 10:1–18**

FURTHER REFLECTION

Write Your blessed name, O Lord, upon my heart,
there to remain so indelibly engraved
that no prosperity,
no adversity shall ever move me from Your love.
Be to me a strong tower of defence,
a comforter in tribulation,
a deliverer in distress,
a very present help in trouble and a guide to heaven
through the many temptations and dangers of this life. Amen.

Thomas à Kempis – German monk and author of The Imitation of Christ
(1379–1471)

SMILE

'If you can't remember people's names, a fairly safe
greeting to anyone over fifty is, 'I hear you've been unwell.'

Anon.

14 UNITY

The *Church Times* reported that, after visiting a church in Melton Mowbray, a child wrote in her school essay, 'The difference between the Church of England and the Methodist Church is that the Methodist Church has double glazing.' If only it were that simple! Sadly, from the outside, those who observe the Christian community don't see a united Church. Instead they behold a confusing array of denominations, all with their distinct styles, theological emphases and traditions. Francis Schaeffer once said, 'We cannot expect the world to believe that the Father sent the Son, that Jesus' claims are true and that Christianity is true, unless the world sees some reality of the oneness of true Christians.'

What do we mean by 'oneness'? I don't think it means 'uniformity'. After all, we don't expect married couples to lose their individual personalities when they become 'one' before God. Despite the fact that they have unique characters and opinions, they learn to share their common objectives, whilst respecting and bearing with each other's idiosyncrasies. Marriage is based upon love and mutual respect. So it should be for Christ's Church!

I despair that some seem to think that Christian unity will only come when all differences have been hammered out. Dream on! Thankfully, we're all different. Church unity comes when, in Christ, Christians recognise their common calling; when they tolerate, love, forgive and respect each other; when they pray together, and roll up their sleeves to share in God's mission without delay. The world desperately needs Christians whose hearts, by God's grace, beat in tune with their Lord's and who celebrate diversity, rather than see it hinder the work of the kingdom.

MAYBE TODAY unity can begin with your openness and obedience to Christ's will.

PRAYER

*Lord, You prayed that Your followers may be one, so the world
may believe. May Your will be done. Amen.*

BIBLE READING

Jesus' prayer for us **John 17:20–26**
Building together **Romans 15:1–7**

FURTHER REFLECTION

May God bless you with discomfort at easy answers, half
truths, and superficial relationships,
so that you may live deep within your heart.
May God bless you with anger at injustice, oppression, and
exploitation of people,
so that you may work for justice, freedom and peace.
May God bless you with tears to shed for those who suffer from
pain, rejection, starvation and war,
so that you may reach out your hand to comfort them and to
turn their pain to joy.
And may God bless you with enough foolishness to believe that
you can make a difference in this world,
so that you can do what others claim cannot be done
to bring justice and kindness to all our children and the poor.
Amen.

A Franciscan benediction – author unknown

SMILE

I'm sure you've heard the hymn that's much loved by
churchgoers, 'We have a gospel to complain!'

Anon.

ONE

A prayer for Christian unity

Almighty Creator,
You alone are our God
– worthy of all our praise and worship.
You gave us the gift of life
and made us to live in community.
You want us to celebrate our diversity,
and to discover that You are a God of unity
who longs for us to be one just as You are one,
so that the world may believe.
With many tongues and yet with one voice,
we worship You together.
We adore You for all that You are
and for the hope that You give
to our broken and fragile world.
We praise You that You have not abandoned us,
but desire us to turn towards Your love,
and seek Your healing and reconciliation in all our
relationships.
You have sent Your Holy Spirit to work in our hearts,
to draw us closer to You and to one another.
We confess, with shame, our stubbornness,
independence and selfishness;
our intolerance, our pride, and our insensitivity towards
others.
We freely admit our lack of desire to live in harmony
with You
and with one another.

Forgive us we pray,
and may we be assured of Your pardon,
through our Saviour Jesus.
May Your grace and mercy permeate our very being;
may we be truly cleansed, renewed,
and remade into our Lord's likeness,
for we ask this prayer in His name,
that we may be living stones,
building upon the Rock for the sake of Your kingdom.
Amen.
TM

BREAKING BAD HABITS

15 THE POWERLESS MONSTER

As a teenager, I enjoyed watching *The Incredible Hulk* on TV. It all started when Dr David Banner, a nuclear physicist, tried to rescue a teenager who'd strayed onto a bomb test site. An accident occurred and thereafter this regular man would suddenly be transformed into a strong green monster and cause havoc. Driven by fury, Banner had no influence over the monster that would come and go without notice; in effect, it mastered him.

Sin is also a terrible master that can dominate the human body. The body isn't bad but, if we're not careful, evil can rule it. As ordinary humans, Christians are in a constant battle against their 'old nature' – they are enslaved by it! Yet, St Paul declares that sin and death no longer have mastery over Jesus because He broke their power on the cross – demonstrated in the resurrection: '… he cannot die again …' (Romans 6:9).

This means sin and death need not oppress us! 'For we know that our old self was crucified with him so that the body of sin might be done away with, that we should no longer be slaves to sin – because anyone who has died has been freed from sin.' (Romans 6:6–7) We must ourselves be 'dead to sin but alive to God in Christ Jesus' (Romans 6:11). In other words, we can claim His holy muscle to help us live victorious lives.

Are you possessed by sin, or gripped by a fear of death?

MAYBE TODAY, unlike David Banner wrestling the Hulk, you can regain control. Jesus can rid you of the monsters that lurk within and you can be free in the mighty strength of the Lord.

PRAYER

Lord Jesus, help me to live for God with a certain hope of heaven. Amen.

BIBLE READING

HE DIED TO SIN ONCE AND FOR ALL **Romans 6:5–11**
IF THE SON SETS YOU FREE **John 8:33–36**

FURTHER REFLECTION

Eternal Light, shine into our hearts,
Eternal Goodness, deliver us from evil,
Eternal Power, be our support,
Eternal Wisdom, scatter the darkness of our ignorance,
Eternal Pity, have mercy upon us;
that with all our heart and mind and soul and strength
we may seek thy face
and be brought by thy infinite mercy to thy holy presence;
through Jesus Christ our Lord.

Alcuin of York – monk, scholar, teacher and poet (735-804)

SMILE

'Courage is fear that has said its prayers.'

Anon.

16 HEY! GOOD LOOKING...

Let's be honest, we're sexual beings and all vulnerable in this respect – even ministers! On a glorious day I stepped out of the church for a breath of fresh air, wearing my 'dog collar'. As I strolled along the High Street, I saw Rod Stewart casually walking towards me arm in arm with his stunning wife, Penny Lancaster (6'1" tall without heels). You can't miss her – especially when she's wearing a mini skirt. As the couple passed by, my head was turned and I walked straight into three ladies from the church. 'We saw you, Tony,' they smiled. 'She's got great legs, hasn't she! Glad to see you're human.' I was so embarrassed and told my wife that I'd been caught out – confident she'd have done the same if she'd passed George Clooney.

Tongue in cheek, a friend once told me that his fiancée had warned him, 'I don't mind you reading the menu, as long as you don't try any other dishes'. Wisely, she was being honest about attraction, but firm about fidelity. Appreciating beauty isn't a sin, but a respected Christian once told me, 'It's how long you look and what you do with your thoughts that's the issue. There's a fine line between appreciation and lust.'

MAYBE TODAY you should be honest about your sexuality too: Recognise temptation for what it is and be conscious of your susceptibility. Don't kid yourself! Honesty is a key step towards purity of heart and behaviour. Beware of degrading or abusing others in your mind. Rather, joyfully appreciate God's gifts in the wholesome way they were intended.

PRAYER

Lord, I thank You for all that 'makes me me', but help me to keep clear of temptation and to appreciate beauty appropriately. Amen.

BIBLE READING
ADULTERY IN THE HEART **Matthew 5:27–30**
WARNING AGAINST ADULTERY **Proverbs 6:20–35**

FURTHER REFLECTION
'I made a covenant with my eyes not to look lustfully at a girl'
(Job 31:1).

Richard J. Foster wrote, 'We must be slow to condemn and
quick to listen to all who are plagued by lust. The temptations
are great in our sex-soaked culture. The distortion of our
sexuality into lust can take a very tangled, twisted route. Only
by the grace of God and the loving support of the Christian
fellowship can our lust-inflamed sexuality be straightened
upright again.'[1]

Creator God, giver of sexuality, may I not feel guilty about
sexual desire itself. Rather, help me to master inappropriate
fantasies and urges and not let them master me. Keep my
heart and mind pure, in the knowledge that I will only truly
be satisfied when I use Your gifts in a wholesome manner and
according to Your will and purpose for me and others. Amen.
TM

SMILE
An eight-year-old girl went to her dad, who was working in
the garden. She asked him, 'Daddy, what's sex?' Her father
was surprised but he decided that if she was old enough to
ask, then she was old enough to get a straight answer. He
proceeded to tell her all about the 'birds and the bees'. When
he'd finished, the little girl looked at him with her mouth wide
open. Curious, her father asked, 'Sweetie, why did you ask this
question?' The little girl replied, 'Mum told me to tell you that
"dinner will be ready in just a couple of secs".'

Anon.

17 HABITS

It was the philosopher, Aristotle, who said, 'We are what we repeatedly do. Excellence, then, is not an act, but a habit.' I find this helpful. The trouble is that my behaviour isn't always good. I develop bad habits! My intentions are good, but temptation, laziness and selfishness often lead to an inappropriate lifestyle. Take driving a car as an example: you have to learn to drive properly to pass your driving test. However, many who passed their test a while ago might *think* they're good drivers, but they've developed bad habits over time. Rather than being 'excellent', it's easy for them to become dangerous without realising it. It has been said, 'Good habits are usually formed; bad habits we fall into.'

MAYBE TODAY is a day for taking a look at those things you repeatedly do. Are you proud of your actions and thoughts? Are there things you could and should change, with God's help? Remember that 'excellence' is a 'good habit'. There's a saying, 'Sow a thought, reap an action; sow an action, reap a habit; sow a habit, reap a character; sow a character, reap a destiny ...'

PRAYER

Lord, keep my thoughts pure, that appropriate actions may follow. Amen.

BIBLE READING

RULES FOR HOLY LIVING **Colossians 3:1–17**
A CALL TO PERSEVERE **Hebrews 10:19–39**

FURTHER REFLECTION

Forgive them all, O Lord:
Our sins of omission and our sins of commission;
The sins of our youth and the sins of our riper years;
The sins of our souls and the sins of our bodies;
Our secret and our more open sins;
Our sins of ignorance and surprise,
And our more deliberate and presumptuous sin;
The sins we have done to please ourselves
And the sins we have done to please others;
The sins we know and remember,
And the sins we have forgotten;
The sins we have striven to hide from others
And the sins by which we have made others offend;
Forgive them, O Lord, forgive them all for His sake,
Who died for our sins and rose for our justification,
And now stands at Thy right hand to make intercession for us,
Jesus Christ our Lord. Amen.

John Wesley – Anglican clergyman, evangelist, and co-founder of the Methodist movement with his brother, Charles (1703–1791)

SMILE

'Habits are like a soft bed – easy to get into but hard to get out of.'

Anon.

18 PAINS IN THE NECK

Some people are *not* easy to love. I'm sure you could name people who are frankly difficult to live with. There are moaners, gossips, hypochondriacs, pessimists and critics; those who are pedantic, rude, boring, inconsiderate, aggressive, and so on. It was Oscar Wilde who said, 'Some cause happiness wherever they go; others whenever they go.' Oh, yes, there are also those without a sense of humour. That's life!

As much as people might wind me up at times, it's good to remember that Jesus loves each one of them – especially the complicated and unlovable. What's more, the Lord wants to love them through me, and you.

MAYBE TODAY is a day for being a blessing and for not crossing the road to avoid your 'pain in the neck'; a day for asking God to nurture a right attitude within; and to see if you can spread a little happiness and raise a smile, rather than complain and become like them in some way.

Paul said, 'The fruit of the Spirit is love, joy, peace, patience, kindness, goodness, faithfulness, gentleness, and self-control.' If you live like this, then people won't take avoiding action when you need them most.

PRAYER

Ever-loving God, help me to be tolerant and big-hearted, lest I become a grouch, rather than a disciple. In Jesus' name. Amen.

BIBLE READING

Patience in the face of suffering **James 5:7–12**
Love each other **1 Thessalonians 4:9–12**

FURTHER REFLECTION

'However much I am at the mercy of the world, I never let myself get lost by brooding over its misery. I hold firmly to the thought that each one of us can do a little to bring some portion of that misery to an end.'

Albert Schweitzer – Medical missionary, theologian, philosopher and musician (1875–1965)

SMILE

A husband and wife came for counselling after fifteen years of marriage. When asked what the problem was, the wife went into a passionate, painful tirade listing every problem they had ever had in the fifteen years they had been married. She went on and on and on: neglect, lack of intimacy, emptiness, loneliness, feeling unloved and unlovable, an entire laundry list of un-met needs she had endured over the course of their marriage. Finally, after allowing this to go on for a sufficient length of time, the therapist got up, walked around the desk and, after asking the wife to stand, embraced and kissed her passionately. The woman shut up and quietly sat down as though in a daze. The therapist turned to the husband and said, 'This is what your wife needs at least three times a week. Can you do this?' The husband thought for a moment and replied, 'Well, I can drop her off here on Mondays and Wednesdays, but on Fridays, I fish.'

Anon.

19 PREJUDICE

A television programme was discussing *prejudice*. As an experiment, a man dressed in his preferred manner, as a Goth (after the 1980s' gothic rock scene which is an off-shoot of the post-punk subculture). The guy had wild hair, black clothes and strange black makeup. He stood in a busy shopping centre and asked people for directions. Most glanced at him and didn't like what they saw. Consequently, they didn't stop, or hastily mumbled a reply, or quickly passed by.

Later on, the same man tied his hair back, wore a suit, and took off his makeup. Standing in the same spot he asked for directions again. There was a total contrast in people's behaviour. Most stopped to try and help him, they stood much closer to him, spoke clearly, and some even offered to walk with him to show the way. The programme was fascinating, but disturbing too. Many of the world's problems are caused by a suspicion and misunderstanding of those who don't appear to be people like us.

MAYBE TODAY is a day for frankly confronting your prejudices. The challenge is to understand your feelings and perceptions, so that you can respond to them in a considered, wholesome and prayerful manner. This means not 'judging a book by its cover', but admitting your ignorance, fears and preconceptions. Then there's the task of understanding people's appearance, race, history, culture and practices, and your instinctive responses to them. Honesty is so important, especially regarding any power you may have over others. People are all different, but we are children of God together and must learn to behave as such.

PRAYER

Thank You, Lord, for Your love and care for all people. Teach me to be more loving and not, consciously or unconsciously, to pre-judge people. Amen.

BIBLE READING

CULTURAL DIFFERENCES **Romans 14:1–12**
A BANQUET FOR ALL PEOPLES **Isaiah 25:6–9**

FURTHER REFLECTION

Be patterns, be examples in all countries, places, islands, nations, wherever you come,
that your carriage and life may preach among all sorts of people, and to them;
then you will come to walk cheerfully over the world, answering that of God in every one.

George Fox – the founder of the Society of Friends, known as the Quakers (1624–1691)

SMILE

'A person should give a lot of thought to sudden decisions.'

Anon.

'If you ASSUME, you'll make an ASS out of U and Me.'

Apparently made famous by an episode of The Odd Couple *aired on 16 February 1973*

20 THE TONGUE

'Sticks and stones may break my bones but words will never hurt me!' Do you remember this saying from your childhood? Well, I don't think it's true. Words *can* hurt. I've spent a fair amount of time pastorally with people who've been badly bruised by lying or unkind words; nagging or angry words; gossip or Chinese whispers; and so on. Just think of the times when you've been the victim of words used maliciously or carelessly. Perhaps you've even spoken inappropriately to someone yourself today – wounding them, whether it was meant intentionally or unintentionally.

A hot-headed woman once told John Wesley, 'My talent is to speak my mind.' Mr Wesley replied, 'Woman, God wouldn't care a bit if you would bury that talent.'

MAYBE TODAY is a day for biting your tongue and recognising what a powerful weapon it can be for good, or evil. Remember that James, the brother of Jesus, spoke of the tongue being like a small spark that can set a forest ablaze (James 3:5). He also said, 'Those who consider themselves religious and yet do not keep a tight reign on their tongues deceive themselves, and their religion is worthless.' (James 1:26, TNIV).

PRAYER

Lord Jesus Your words are true, loving and healing. May I remember today that ' … even a fool may be thought wise and intelligent if he stays quiet and keeps his mouth shut' (Prov. 17:28, GNB). Amen.

BIBLE READING

Taming the tongue **James 3:1–12**
A time for everything **Ecclesiastes 3:1–8**

FURTHER REFLECTION

Tongues are funny things to look at, Lord.
Who'd have thought that such a peculiar part of my anatomy
could be so powerful.
Your servant James likened it to a fire –
it can rage uncontrolled and render religion worthless;
my tongue can curse or bless!
Jesus, I want You to be Master of all of me,
including my tongue.
By Your Spirit grant me self-control
and wisdom in all I do today,
that I may know when to speak
and when to draw circles in the sand quietly. Amen.[2]

TM

SMILE

Lord, fill my mouth with worthwhile stuff
and nudge me when I've said enough.

Anon.

21 GRATITUDE

One of the first things we teach a child is the importance of saying, 'thank you'. Yet, it surprises me how many adults seem to forget those two important little words. My wife, Frances, thinks that car drivers are a classic example – especially when they fail to offer an acknowledgement after others have given way to them.

This reminds me of the story of a little girl who went to a birthday party. When her Mum dropped her at the home where the action was taking place, she said, 'Whatever happens, you must remember to say 'thank you' to your host when you leave the party. Don't forget, will you?' Well, the party was splendid and Mum returned to pick up her daughter. As Mums tend to do, the first question she asked her daughter as they made their way to the car was, 'Did you remember to say thank you?' Sheepishly her daughter replied, 'No I didn't.' 'What? Didn't you listen to me?' said Mum. To which a little voice said, 'The girl in front did, but the lady said "Don't mention it", so I didn't!'

MAYBE TODAY is a day for endeavouring to live with gratitude in your heart and to express it with your lips: gratitude to your family and friends, gratitude to your colleagues, gratitude to others, and gratitude to God. Just because others don't live thankfully, doesn't mean that you should do the same. The American journalist and feminist, Gloria Steinem, said, 'Silent gratitude isn't much good to anyone.'
So, thank you for reading this thought!

PRAYER

Gracious God, I'm sorry for taking You for granted and for failing to express love and gratitude in response to all You have given. Thank You for expressing your love and encouragement. May

Your Holy Spirit enable me to reflect Your nature, that others may know the wonder of Your love and be inspired to worship and adore You, through Jesus Christ, our Lord. Amen.

BIBLE READING

THE IMPORTANCE OF SAYING THANK YOU **Luke 17:11–19**
GIVE THANKS TO THE LORD FOR HE IS GOOD **Psalm 136**

FURTHER REFLECTION

Now thank we all our God,
With hearts and hands and voices,
Who wondrous things has done,
In whom his world rejoices;
Who from our mother's arms
Has blessed us on our way
With countless gifts of love,
And still is ours today.

Martin Rinkart – German clergyman and hymn-writer (1586–1649)
Tr. Catherine Winkworth – English translator (1827–1878)

SMILE
'The atheist's most embarrassing moment is when he feels profoundly thankful for something but can't think of anybody to thank for it.'

Mary Ann Vincent – British born American actress (1818–1887)

COME TO THE LIGHT

In the beginning God said 'Let there be light'.
The light shines in the darkness, but the darkness has
not overcome it.

This is the light that God works by,
To shape and mould each planet, star;
A grand design, a project vast.
This is the light that God works by,
To bring to birth the little things
Dormouse, ant, creatures tiny-winged
But darkness isn't far away,
Death, destruction, creeping in.
Such beauty, yet such pain.
The flame flickers!
Lord, don't let the light go out!
Save your world!

Come to the light – I am there,
I will transform, preserve, renew.
My spirit's flame and energy
Brings healing, strength and life.

This is the light that God works by
To bring to life your heart and mind, your body, soul.
You are no less a work of art
than any creature God has made,
in eye and hand, in tongue and toe,
in thought and action, reason, dream.
But darkness mars your image, Lord,
In greed, abuse and jealous pride.

Such goodness, yet such sin.
The flame flickers!
Lord, don't let the light go out!
Save your people!

Come to the light – I am there,
I will renew, preserve, transform –
My spirit's flame and energy
Brings healing, strength and life.

This is the light that God works by:
The Jesus light, the light for all
Which saves and cares and serves in love.
This is the light that God works by,
Shining through – in me and you.
And though we may not feel as though
We're good enough to take this on;
And though we may in shadow walk,
Shadows of fear and grief and pain,
Yet still he calls and draws us near
To the light, to the spirit, the flame of life.
My flame burns low!
Save me, save us, save all.

Come to the light – I am there,
I will renew, preserve, transform –
My spirit's flame and energy
Brings healing, strength and life.

Christine F. Watts
Used with permission. Copyright © Christine F. Watts October 2003

ACTIONS
SPEAK
LOUDER

22 VERBAL ABUSE

An inconsiderate driver had parked across a pavement forcing a dad to step into the road in order to pass with his little girl in a pushchair. Understandably, the man was not happy with the motorist. He was protective towards his daughter who had been exposed to danger on a very busy street by the thoughtless obstruction.

However, as the man remonstrated with the van driver, his voice became increasingly raised and he poured out a torrent of vicious four-letter words and other vulgarities. The youngster looked frightened and tried to interrupt by asking why he was shouting. Her father's reply wasn't much better! I watched the child being pushed off vigorously into the distance. She was evidently confused and upset.

Children are vulnerable to being hurt by our unthinking words as well as our actions. The little girl's dad thought he was shielding her from harm, yet in reality he had put her at risk of being traumatised and scarred by his frightening and abusive language.

MAYBE TODAY you could reflect on the damage you can cause through a moment of unrestrained temper, or by failing to control your tongue in other ways. Perhaps this story could be a reminder that all adults have a responsibility to ensure that children are safeguarded from every kind of abuse. Moreover, if you take steps to protect children, make certain that well-intentioned actions are appropriate.

PRAYER

Word of Life, help me to protect the vulnerable and, in doing so, let my tongue be used constructively, rather than as a thoughtless weapon. In Jesus' name and for His sake. Amen.

BIBLE READING

ARGUING ON THE ROAD **Mark 9:33–37**
DO NOT EXASPERATE YOUR CHILDREN **Ephesians 6:1–4**

FURTHER REFLECTION

Child protection in churches: 'Children need to be honoured as present members of the churches, not just because of their potential to be adult Christians in the future. An emphasis on parental responsibilities rather than an authoritarian view of parental rights may also help to create a context in which children are more valued and respected.' [1]

Patrick Parkinson – a Professor of Law at the University of Sydney

SMILE

'Everybody knows how to raise children, except the people who have them.' [2]

P.J. O'Rourke – American political satirist, journalist, and writer (1947–)

23 FAITH IN ACTION

'Hypocrites!' Sadly, those outside the Christian community
often feel able to pin this label on churchgoers. However unfair
I consider this accusation to be, it challenges me to take a good
look at my faith and life.

It was St Francis of Assisi who said, 'Preach the Gospel at
all times. If necessary use words.' In other words, Christians
must earn the right to be heard. The best way to do this is by
practising what we'd like to preach.

MAYBE TODAY you could consider whether or not your
heart is driven by God's active love. If not, people may not hear
what you say about your faith, because *who* you are shouts too
loudly! Nevertheless, if with the help of God's Spirit you change
the way you behave, then His holiness in you will communicate
powerfully. Someone once said, 'The way from God to a human
heart, is through a human heart.' Perhaps that's why people
remember St Francis more for his actions than his words.

PRAYER

*Faithful God of truth, help me to live out my faith with integrity,
for Jesus' sake. Amen.*

BIBLE READING

LET US NOT LOVE WITH WORDS AND TONGUE BUT WITH
ACTIONS **1 John 3:11–24**
SAVED BY GRACE AND NOT WORKS **Ephesians 2:1–10**

FURTHER REFLECTION

'John Wesley's Rule' – There is no evidence that John wrote this, but it is attributed to him:

Do all the good you can,
By all the means you can,
In all the ways you can,
In all the places you can,
At all the times you can,
To all the people you can,
As long as ever you can.

John Wesley – Anglican clergyman, evangelist, and co-founder of the Methodist movement with his brother, Charles (1703–1791)

Most High, Glorious God,
enlighten the darkness of our minds.
Give us a right faith, a firm hope and a perfect charity,
so that we may always and in all things act according to Your
Holy Will. Amen.

St Francis of Assisi – Roman Catholic friar and founder of the Order of the Friars Minor, known as the Franciscans (1182–1226)

SMILE

'A good sermon should be like a mini-skirt: short enough to be interesting, yet long enough to cover the subject.'

Anon.

24 MISSION POSSIBLE

I confess that I get increasingly irritated by people who say their faith is a 'private thing' – between them and God. I understand it's true in one sense, but a Christian's individual relationship with their Creator should overflow into service. The followers of Jesus should share His mission and help establish God's kingdom. We are interdependent and made to be in relationship with each other and our Maker (Father, Son and Holy Spirit – the loving community of the Godhead).

I can't watch my TV and the graphic and devastating pictures of suffering, poverty and injustice around the world, whilst basking in a luxurious 'private' faith. A very public world is crying out for my concern and to react by serving my neighbours generously – whoever they may be. God is love and, made in His image, I must let love shake me out of my comfort zone and place me alongside the vulnerable, broken and grieving.

I remember interviewing Mark Perrott, CEO of the Catalyst Trust, who was telling me about their Urban Mission Toolkit. Mark told how people are being trained for mission in difficult areas. He said, 'We are building local response-ability with ordinary people to do extra-ordinary things in tough places … because love is a verb!'

MAYBE TODAY you can ensure your faith isn't passive. May your good intentions become a reality – a blessing to those in need! St John of the Cross said, 'Mission is putting love where love is not.'

PRAYER

God of Love, may I be ever aware of the need around me, and ever-ready to act in Your name with Your sustaining help and guidance. Amen.

BIBLE READING

GOD'S LOVE AND OURS **1 John 4:7–21**
A FRAGRANT OFFERING FOR THOSE IN NEED
Philippians 4:14–18

FURTHER REFLECTION

We thank You, Good Shepherd,
that You have kept us safe in Your care and provided for us;
You have blessed us with the gift of life
and sustained us through all our joys and sorrows;
You have saved us and we are no longer lost, but found by Your grace!
Come and fill your hungry lambs
and, in Your mercy, receive all we offer to You,
that our offering of love in action
may further the work of Your kingdom;
to the praise and glory of Your holy name. Amen.

TM

SMILE

What does love mean? Elaine, aged 5, answered,
'Love is when Mummy gives Daddy the best bit of chicken.'

Anon.

25 GOD'S INSTRUMENTS

I have a passion for listening to music and my iPod is a good friend when travelling to work. My taste is broad, from modern pop to jazz and classical. However, I'm a listener and not a music-maker. I deeply regret never having learnt to play a musical instrument when younger. I had the choice but, with hindsight, I made the wrong one. Perhaps one day I can rectify the matter – even if it means asking the angels to teach me the harp in heaven!

The word 'instrument' can be used to describe an object – a weapon, tool or channel – that is used to accomplish a particular purpose. Paul reminds his Roman readers that they can use their bodies as weapons of wickedness, or offer them to God as channels through which a harmonious godly relationship can flow. He says, 'Do not offer the parts of your body to sin, as instruments of wickedness, but rather offer yourselves to God ...' (Romans 6:13).

Are you grasping God's purpose for your life? We often know instinctively what's right. Even in my non-musical state, I still know the difference between a badly played violin, for example, and a sweet sounding one!

MAYBE TODAY Paul offers a stark choice: Choose badly and you'll repeatedly use your body to sin – possibly preventing God from using you. Alternatively, be wise and offer yourself as God's tool, learning the art of being in tune with godly living. Don't wait to rectify things in heaven – that may be too late!

PRAYER

Lord Jesus, help me not only to listen, but to put holy living into practice each day. Amen.

BIBLE READING

OFFER YOURSELVES TO GOD AND NOT SIN **Romans 6:1–14**
OFFERING A SACRIFICE OF PRAISE **Hebrews 13:15–16**

FURTHER REFLECTION

To you, O Lord, let us direct our eyes.
To you let us offer our hands.
To you let us bow the knee.
To you let us sacrifice our life.
To you let us come at last
and in you let us rest forever. Amen.

Attributed to Sir Walter Raleigh – the Renaissance poet, explorer, historian and one of Queen Elizabeth's favourite courtiers (1552–1618)

'Music is an echo of the innumerable voices of Eternity.'

Sir Thomas Beecham, 2nd Baronet – English conductor and impresario (1879–1961)

SMILE

'A musician is walking past a bank when he sees a sign saying, "Musician bank loans. 2%". This is an incredible deal and the musician rushes inside to borrow some money. He goes to the cashier and asks, "Can I borrow £2,000 at your 2% musician's rate?" The cashier replies, "I'm sorry sir. 2% isn't the interest rate. It's your chance of actually getting a loan."'

Anon.

26 LEAVING OUR MARK

Consider this list: William Wilberforce, Mother Teresa of Calcutta, Martin Luther King Jr, Elizabeth Fry, Desmond Tutu, Florence Nightingale, Dr Barnardo, John Wesley and Eric Liddell. These are just a few well-known Christians. All of them have been 'movers and shakers' in various ways. No one could say their faith was dead. Why? Well, they've certainly left their mark on the world.

I'm reminded of a story about a miller who finished work with his overalls covered in flour. As he edged his way home through crowded streets and shops, he left his mark on everyone he touched. When I think of Christians who've had an impact on my life, it's because they've had a 'living faith': a faith that is alive and certainly not dead, or dormant.

William Booth, the founder of the Salvation Army, said, 'Faith and works should travel side by side, step answering to step, like the legs of men walking. First faith, and then works; and then faith again, and then works again – until you can scarcely distinguish which is one and which is the other.' Hence, as the classical scholar, Edith Hamilton, wrote, 'Faith is not belief. Belief is passive. Faith is active.'

MAYBE TODAY, if you feel your belief is dead or dying, get on with living out Jesus' teaching and hopefully the heart will start pumping again!

PRAYER

Gracious Lord Jesus, by Your Spirit, nurture a living faith within me that, wherever I go, Your work may have an impact. Amen.

BIBLE READING

FAITH AND DEEDS **James 2:14–26**
JESUS MAKES AN IMPACT **Matthew 13:53–58**

FURTHER REFLECTION

Lord Jesus, I give you my hands to do your work.
I give you my feet to go your way.
I give you my eyes to see as you do.
I give you my tongue to speak your words.
I give you my mind that you may think in me.
I give you my spirit that you may pray in me.
Above all, I give you my heart
that you may love in me your Father and all humanity.
I give you my whole self that you may grow in me,
so that it is you, Lord Jesus,
who live and work and pray in me. Amen.

The Grail Prayer (England)

SMILE

'If you want to know what a person is really like,
put them in a position of authority.'

Anon.

27 MORE THAN TICKING A BOX

My 'IN' tray is frequently inundated with research surveys. It's trendy to pick the brains of busy people (making them even busier) by issuing forms to be completed. Someone ought to research how much time people spend filling out questionnaires! Tick boxes often make the task easier. 'What is your religion?' is often asked, followed by various options. It's painless to mark a piece of paper. Hence in the 2001 census, about 72% ticked to say they were Christian, but only about half of Britons said they actually believed in God! By 2005, the harsh reality was that only 6.8% attended church in Britain.

True Christianity demands dedication and it's only the committed who'll foster a living faith with meaning, purpose and hope. This requires more than ticking a box and more than an intellectual acknowledgement of doctrine. Devout Jews daily affirmed their belief in 'one' God (Deuteronomy 6:4), but James declares that even 'the demons believe – and shudder' (James 2:19). This was the case in the New Testament (Acts 16:17). Yet, the demons didn't have 'saving faith', for there's no evidence of love, trust or goodness of heart. Equally, if you tick the boxes of 'good works' alone, that won't save you either!

MAYBE TODAY, in order to indicate authentic faith, you could *demonstrate* that you mean business with God. I believe that if you do this you'll never need to shudder!

PRAYER

Holy God, lest I be 'ticked off' by You, embrace me in Your love and mercy, and help me to serve Christ faithfully every day. Amen.

BIBLE READING

PAUL AND SILAS IN PRISON **Acts 16:16–40**
LOVE THE LORD YOUR GOD **Deuteronomy 6:3–9**

FURTHER REFLECTION

Fix thou our steps, O Lord,
that we stagger not at the uneven motions of the world,
but steadily go on to our glorious home;
neither censuring our journey by the weather we meet with,
nor turning out of the way for anything that befalls us.
The winds are often rough,
And our own weight presses us downwards.
Reach forth, O Lord, thy saving hand, and speedily deliver us.
Teach us, O Lord,
to use this transitory life as pilgrims returning to their beloved
home;
that we may take what our journey requires,
and not think of settling in a foreign country. Amen.

*John Wesley – Anglican clergyman, evangelist, and co-founder of the Methodist
movement with his brother, Charles (1703–1791)*

SMILE

'Three vicars were having lunch together. One said, 'You
know, since summer started I've been having trouble with
bats at church. I've tried everything – noise, spray, cats –
nothing seems to scare them away.' Another said, 'Yes, me
too. I've got hundreds living in my belfry. I've even had the
place fumigated, and they still won't go away.' The third
said, 'I baptised all mine, and made them members of the
church … Haven't seen one of them back since!'[3]

Anon.

28 TIME

'How are you?' someone enquired thoughtfully. My reply was spontaneous, 'Life is full!' I wasn't using the word 'full' in the same sense as Jesus saying, 'I have come that they may have life, and have it to the full' (John 10:10). There's a world of difference between 'busyness' and a 'fulfilled life with meaning and purpose'.

What have you got planned for today? When the preacher George Whitfield was asked what he'd do if he knew Christ would return in three days, he replied, 'I would do just what I have scheduled to do'. Could you say the same? If I'm honest, I couldn't be as categorical. There are often things I do that I shouldn't, and other things that could be done that I put off to a future date. Another preacher, John Wesley, said: 'I am not careful for what may be a hundred years hence. He who governed the world before I was born shall take care of it, likewise when I am dead. My part is to improve the present moment.'

MAYBE TODAY is one for improving the present moment and being prayerful about the day ahead.

PRAYER

Lord of life, all time comes from You and I am a steward of all You have entrusted to me. May I live purposefully today and resist being swept along by others, or my own thoughtlessness. Amen.

BIBLE READING

YOUNG SAMUEL CALLED FOR A PURPOSE **1 Samuel 3:1–21**
PARABLE OF THE TALENTS **Matthew 25:14–30**

FURTHER REFLECTION

God has created me to do Him some definite service;
He has committed some work to me which He has not
committed to another. I have my mission – I may never
know it in this life, but I shall be told it in the next. I am a
link in a chain, a bond of connection between persons. He
has not created me for naught. I shall do good, I shall do His
work. I shall be an angel of peace, a preacher of the truth in
my own place while not intending it – if I do but keep His
Commandments. Therefore I will trust Him. Whatever,
wherever I am, I can never be thrown away. If I am in sickness,
my sickness may serve Him; in perplexity, my perplexity may
serve Him; if I am in sorrow, my sorrow may serve Him. He
does nothing in vain. He knows what He is about. He may take
away my friends. He may throw me among strangers. He may
make me feel desolate, make my spirits sinks, hide my future
from me – still He knows what He is about.

Venerable John Henry (Cardinal) Newman – Leader of the Oxford Movement.
Eventually converted to the Roman Catholic Church – theologian and author
(1801–1890)

SMILE

'One of life's mysteries: why is it when people retire and
time is no longer of such great importance, they often get
presented with a watch?'

Anon.

'Time and Tide wait for no man, but time always stands
still for a woman of thirty.'

Robert Frost (Lee) – American poet (1874–1963)

MAYBE TODAY...

Maybe today...
    the doorbell will ring
    and a smiling face
    will light up the day for me.

Maybe today...
    the phone will ring
    and a happy voice
    will ask "How are you?"

Maybe today...
    this dark, dark cloud
    will lift and this grief and pain
    will be eased.

Maybe today...
    the scars will heal
    and I'll find the strength
    to leave and change my future.

Maybe today...
    is the day to make a difference,
    a day for others
    to feel God's care,
    through me, through you. Maybe?

OUT OF THE COMFORT ZONE

29 NO MORE POOR AMONG YOU ...

It's both a privilege and a challenge to work in Westminster. For example, there's the reality of poverty in the midst of wealth alongside London's corridors of power. As I make my way to the comfort of my office, I'm made uncomfortable as I pass people sleeping in cardboard boxes along Victoria Street. I'm starkly reminded of the world's inequalities and my failure to address adequately the root causes of poverty and injustice. Moreover, as I watch the predictable horrors of global poverty on the nightly news, I'm haunted by words from Deuteronomy, 'However, there should be no poor among you, for in the land the LORD your God is giving you to possess as your inheritance, he will richly bless you, if only you fully obey the LORD your God ...' (Deuteronomy 15:4–5).

Frequently, my eyes also fall upon the ten statues above the West Door of Westminster Abbey representing the Christian martyrs of the twentieth century. The French *Richemont limestone* figures proclaim powerful messages. One carving depicts Oscar Romero, the fourth Roman Catholic Bishop of San Salvador who was committed to the poor and persecuted. He was assassinated for speaking out about ongoing human rights violations during his country's civil war. He was called a 'Shepherd of the Poor', and once quoted Bishop Camara, 'When I feed the poor, they call me a saint. When I ask why they are poor, they call me a communist.'[1]

MAYBE TODAY you could leave your comfort zone to ask more 'why' questions. Don't worry about people's defensive arguments. After all, ultimately, it's what God thinks that really matters.

PRAYER

God of all, help me to find ways to help and protect the poor and powerless, believing that with You change is possible. Amen.

BIBLE READING

THE YEAR FOR CANCELLING DEBTS **Deuteronomy 15:1–11**
JESUS GIVES HIS MANIFESTO **Luke 4:14–21**

FURTHER REFLECTION

Here are some now famous words from an address given by Oscar Romero a few months before he died:
'I have frequently been threatened with death. I must say that, as a Christian, I do not believe in death without resurrection. If they kill me, I will be resurrected in the hearts of the Salvadoran people.'

He also said on 4 March 1979:
'If we are worth anything, it is not because we have more money or more talent, or more human qualities.
Insofar as we are worth anything, it is because we are grafted on to Christ's life, his cross and resurrection.
That is a person's measure.'

Oscar Romero – Latin American Archbishop (1917–1980)

SMILE

'The poorest people in this world are those who think only in terms of profit.'

Anon.

30 EASY LIFE?

It was the American rock star, Bruce Springsteen, who once said, 'Success makes life easier. It doesn't make living easier.'

In a culture that seems preoccupied and dominated with personality, it's worth remembering that 'success' isn't everything. What is success, anyway? Could it be that God's understanding is different from our own? The rich and famous may give the outward impression that they've got life all sewn-up, but both fame and fortune bring with them responsibility and accountability. Moreover, many of the problems the 'stars' face are very ordinary. Believe it or not, even superstars are human!

MAYBE TODAY you could remember that living will never be plain sailing – whoever we are. Even Jesus, the Son of God, never had an easy ride. What's more, He didn't promise one for His followers. Instead, He said: 'If anyone would come after me, he must deny himself and take up his cross and follow me' (Matthew 16:24) and 'Come to me, all you who are weary and burdened, and I will give you rest' (Matthew 11:28).

Maybe finding meaning, purpose and peace in the midst of life's challenges is the real key to success – however famous you are.

PRAYER

God of life and love, help me to discern what is most important, and to live courageously and purposefully, wherever I find myself. In Jesus' name. Amen.

BIBLE READING

THE COST OF FOLLOWING JESUS **Matthew 16:24–28**
WHAT TO DO IF LIFE ISN'T EASY **Habakkuk 3:16–19**

FURTHER REFLECTION

Eternal Father, you said, 'Let us make humankind to our own image and likeness.' Thus you were willing to share with us your own greatness. You gave us the intellect to share your truth. You gave us wisdom to share your goodness. And you gave us the free will to love that which is true and just. Why did you so dignify us? It was because you looked upon us, and fell in love with us. It was a love which first prompted you to create us; and it was love which caused you to share with us your truth and goodness. Yet your heart must break when you see us turn against you. You must weep when you see us abusing our intellect in pursuit of that which is false. You must cry with pain when we distort our wisdom in order to justify evil. But you never desert us. Out of the same love that caused you to create us, you have now sent your only Son to save us. He is your perfect image and likeness, and so through him we can be restored to your image and likeness.'

St Catherine of Siena – Italian scholastic philosopher and theologian (1347–1380)

SMILE

'The only place where success comes before work is in a dictionary.'

Vidal Sassoon – top name in British hairdressing during the 60s (1928–)

'Success that goes to a person's head usually pays a short visit.'

Anon.

31 SHOPPING

Are you an 'exocet' or a 'moocher'? When it comes to shopping my son and I are 'exocets': we know what we're looking for; we sort out our navigation, then go and get what's on the list. Hopefully, the mission is accomplished in the shortest time possible. My wife and daughter find this frustrating. They are 'moochers' and like to browse aimlessly, and take pleasure in window shopping.

Now, whether an 'exocet' or 'moocher', our decision making is swayed by our budget, our needs, and our wants. What's more, we're all suckers for a good bargain and manipulated by advertising. Sadly, these are all subtle and powerful influences – more so, regrettably, than justice, poverty and the environment, which are surely the pressing issues today.

MAYBE TODAY is the day for a spending review? Why do you buy what you buy? What impact does your shopping have on others and this fragile world? Are you prepared to pay a bit more as a long-term investment in people and this world? For me, it may mean spending more time seeking out fairly-traded and environmentally-friendly products. For 'moochers', a more strategic approach may be in order, to aim for ethical retailers and to choose 'trade justice' before you leave for the shops.

PRAYER

Righteous God, of justice and compassion, may my faith hit me where it really hurts when shopping … even in my wallet! Amen.

BIBLE READING

THE LORD'S JUDGMENT ON ISRAEL **Amos 2:6–7a**
JESUS CALLS US TO PRIORITISE **Matthew 6:25–34**

FURTHER REFLECTION

Take a look at the Fairtrade Foundation website:
www.fairtrade.org.uk

The Fairtrade Foundation has licensed over 3,000 Fairtrade certified products for sale through retail and catering outlets in the UK.

The UK market is doubling in value every two years, and in 2007 reached an estimated retail value of £493 million. The UK is one of the world's leading Fairtrade markets, with more products and more awareness of Fairtrade than anywhere else. Around 20% of roast and ground coffee, and 20% of bananas sold in the UK are now Fairtrade.

SMILE

'I went to the butcher's the other day and I bet him fifty quid that he couldn't reach the meat off the top shelf. He said, 'No, the steaks are too high.'

Tommy Cooper – British comedian and magician (1921–1984)

32 CAMELS AND NEEDLES

A Jewish proverb came to mind after I had my wallet stolen: 'If you want to know what a man is really like, take notice how he acts when he loses money.'

Admit it or not, money can possess us. Paul said, 'For the love of money is a root of all kinds of evil' (1 Timothy 6:10). That's why John Wesley, the founder of Methodism, said, 'Earn all you can. Save all you can. Give all you can.' For him, money wasn't wrong, but it should be handled properly and with care for others.

Jesus challenged the Jewish idea that riches were a sign of God's blessing. He turned social order on its head; radical even for His disciples. He said, 'It is easier for a camel to go through the eye of a needle than for a rich man to enter the kingdom of God' (Mark 10:25). The message wasn't that rich people couldn't be saved, but that it would be 'hard'; impossible, in fact, without God's grace. That's why He humorously talks about a camel, the largest animal in Palestine, trying to pass through the eye of a sewing needle. Ludicrous! And so it is for those who trust in their own wealth to enter God's kingdom.

MAYBE TODAY I should remember Jesus said, 'You cannot serve both God and Money' (Matthew 6:24). I conclude with an English proverb: 'Riches serve a wise man but command a fool.'

PRAYER

Gracious God, may my generosity be a blessing to others, a blessing to You, and a blessing to me eternally, through Jesus my Saviour. Amen.

BIBLE READING

GOD AND MONEY **Matthew 6:19–24**
LOVE OF MONEY **1 Timothy 6:3–10**

FURTHER REFLECTION

Awesome God, in You we put our faith
and not without reason.
You are our provider and sustainer;
You are our deliverer and healer;
You are the lover of our souls.
We offer our gifts in gratitude and with thanksgiving.
Accept our money and our lives lived in Your service,
for the furtherance of Your kingdom,
in the name of Christ our Lord and Saviour.

TM

SMILE

'All I ask is a chance to prove that money can't make me happy.'

Spike Milligan – Irish/British comedic genius, writer, musician, and poet.
He played Eccles in The Goons (1918–2002)

'We are here on earth to do good to others; what the others are here for I have no idea.'

W.H. Auden – Anglo-American poet and essayist (1907–1973)

33 RAISING THE POOR

'My problems would be solved if I could just win the lottery!'
Well, I've never won – not surprising really, since I've never
bought a ticket. Leaving aside the gambling issue, most people
find wealth appealing. However, Jesus points out the huge
responsibility it brings. Think of the imbalance when millions
are in abject poverty. The rich get richer, whilst the poor are
mostly forgotten – left to fend for themselves.

The preacher, Jim Wallis, points out that one in every sixteen
New Testament verses relates to wealth and poverty, yet we
rarely hear sermons on the subject.[2] Could our lack of concern
for material poverty be symptomatic of our spiritual deficiency?
Relatively speaking, I'm rich compared to the world's majority.

Psalm 113:7–8 reads, 'He raises the poor from the dust and
lifts the needy from the ash heap; he seats them with princes,
with the princes of their people.' This echoes the Song of
Hannah in 1 Samuel 2:8. Our exalted God graciously stoops
to lift the poor. He acts to rescue the wretched from their
existence, restoring their honour and dignity, elevating them
to a place of honour with princes. The 'ash heap' refers to the
shelter of the village dump: rather like the rubbish tips in Brazil
where the destitute scrape for their livelihood. God acts to
make them spiritually rich!

MAYBE TODAY you could reflect on Proverbs 14 verse 31:
'He who oppresses the poor shows contempt for their Maker,
but whoever is kind to the needy honours God.'

PRAYER

*Liberating God, lift me today. Help me to use what I have to bless
others in need. Amen.*

BIBLE READING

PRAISE TO THE LORD WHO STOOPS **Psalm 113**
HANNAH'S PRAYER **1 Samuel 2:1-10**

FURTHER REFLECTION

We bring before you, O Lord,
the troubles and perils of peoples and nations,
the frustration of prisoners and captives,
the anguish of the bereaved,
the needs of refugees,
the helplessness of the weak,
the despondency of the weary,
the failing powers of the aged
and the hopelessness of the starving.
O Lord, draw near to each,
for the sake of Jesus Christ our Lord.

After St Anselm of Canterbury – Italian clergyman, scholastic philosopher and theologian (1033–1109)

'Poverty is no disgrace, but ignorance is.'
Anon.

SMILE

'I have no money at all: I live, or am supposed to live, on a few francs a day … Like dear St Francis of Assisi I am wedded to Poverty: but in my case the marriage is not a success.'

Oscar Wilde – witty Irish playwright, poet and author (1854–1900)

34 GREEN POLICY

Imagine someone spending time and effort painting a beautiful picture, only to have it vandalised by some inconsiderate and cruel person. How do you think the artist would feel? I think I'd be distraught. If that's the case, I wonder how God feels about the way this thoughtless and selfish generation is, at times, destroying His creation. Bishop Trevor Huddleston once said, 'We forget that this is God's world, created and sustained by him, and not ours "to do with what we like". We must recover, before it is too late, a Christian theology of Creation.'

The Leadership Team of Methodist Central Hall, Westminster, has adopted a *Green Policy*. This is an endeavour to help our church play its part in caring for the environment. There's much work to do, but at least we've made a start and a commitment to be 'stewards' of creation. Tim Cooper writes, 'In recent times this concept of stewardship is often mistakenly understood solely in the context of financing the Church … It has become too closely identified with raising money for the needs of the Church, instead of using appropriately *all* of the resources which God has entrusted to us – our time, energy and money, and especially the gift of God's creation.'[3]

MAYBE TODAY is a day for introducing a *Green Policy* into your life or household. This is for God's sake, for your own benefit, and with concern for future generations.

Ponder this thought that was coined by twentieth-century environmentalist David Brower (possibly a native Indian proverb): 'We do not inherit the earth from our ancestors, we are borrowing it from our children.'

Being *green* is not a trendy fad; it's about living responsibly and considerately.

PRAYER

Creator God, help me to live carefully and purposefully every day, in Jesus' name. Amen.

BIBLE READING

ADAM AND EVE – EDEN'S CARETAKERS **Genesis 2:15–25**
IN AWE OF THE CREATOR **Psalm 8**

FURTHER REFLECTION

Enjoy the earth gently
Enjoy the earth gently
For if the earth is spoiled
It cannot be repaired.
Enjoy the earth gently.

West African Poem

SMILE

'How is it one careless match can start a forest fire, but it takes a whole box to start a barbecue?'

Anon.

35 CONSERVATION

It's strange that there can sometimes be a water shortage when it's pouring down with rain. Nevertheless, that was the case when I first wrote this reflection: people in the South East of England were being told that our water was running out, literally running out, from broken pipes of an aging infrastructure, and from taps that were being left running in homes unnecessarily! The call was to preserve scarce resources. What's more, we were asked not to waste gas and electricity – by turning off the TV, rather than leaving it on standby, for example.

MAYBE TODAY you could take conservation seriously. I believe Christians should be God's caretakers: we are entrusted as 'stewards of His creation'. If that's the case, our Creator cares about how we look after His world, and each other. So, being a conserver of natural resources is not an option, but a holy obligation.

The trouble is, looking at the low level of huge reservoirs I'm tempted to believe that my efforts won't make a difference. Yet, I'm reminded of a quote from Mother Teresa: we may think our efforts are a drop in the ocean, but 'the ocean is made up of a lot of little drops'.

PRAYER

Creator God, help me to be a loving caretaker of the world's resources, rather than being carefree and selfish. May this be part of the worship I offer You. Amen.

BIBLE READING

How many are Your works, O Lord! **Psalm 104**
The supremacy of Christ **Colossians 1:15–23**

FURTHER REFLECTION

Deep peace of the running wave to you –
Deep peace of the flowing air to you –
Deep peace of the quiet earth to you –
Deep peace of the shining stars to you –
Deep peace of the Prince of peace to you.
May the road rise to meet you
May the wind be always at your back.
May the sun shine warm upon your face.
May the rains fall softly upon your fields.
Until we meet again –
May God hold you in the hollow of His hand.

An Old Gaelic Blessing

SMILE

'Let me get this straight,' said the student who was being taught 'The Big Bang' theory of how the universe came into existence, 'first there was nothing at all and then it exploded.'

Anon.

COUNTDOWN

Would you believe it? How could this be?
Five little words – "In the beginning God created…"
And the universe exploded into wonder and beauty and
order.
All it took were
Four little words – "Let there be light"
And fruitful earth was dressed in splendour,
sky was jewel-filled,
eagles soared and wrens hip-hopped,
while dolphins danced and whales ploughed the deep.
All was abundance and glory – but not enough, said
God,
so four and six and eight legged creatures joined in the
fun.
But supreme and reflecting the glory of God,
to paradise came woman and man.

Would you believe it? How could this be?
For murder, waste, and blame and hate defaced the glory
and brought disgrace.
Yet hope had not ended and hard work began,
for God came to paradise – with outstretched hands;
with miracle and story He told the truth, and walked the
way;
renewing, transforming, saving, loving, until –
with hammer and nail and tide of blood
He secured our destiny.

From the brutal tree, His
Three little words – "It is finished" –
were the victory cry for you and me.
In the place of disgrace came "the grace that heals and
forgives",
In the place of death stood "the love that lives".
Would you believe it? How could this be?

Now two little words echo down through the years –
"Follow me, follow me".
Your choice, your choice – to begin the journey or
recommit
to the way of faith, of hope, of love, the way this world
could be.
Your heart is God's home and your 'Yes' is
the one little word He's waiting to hear.

Five, four, three, two, one – would you believe it?

GOD'S MYSTERIOUS PRESENCE

36 GOD IS WATCHING

Children lined up for lunch in the cafeteria of a Catholic primary school. At the head of the table was a large pile of apples. A nun had written a note on a piece of blue card beside the heap which read, 'Take only one! God is watching.' Moving through the line to the other end of the table, a small boy found a large stack of chocolate chip cookies. He wrote this note on the tablecloth: 'Take all you want, God is watching the apples.'

It's a sobering thought that God is looking in more than one place. Many will remember a song that Sir Cliff Richard recorded, written by Julie Gold, in 1985. It was called, 'From a distance'. It suggests God is surveying this world. Let me quote from it: '… God is watching us, God is watching us from a distance.' It's a good song, but the truth is that God isn't far away from us at all.

MAYBE TODAY you could remember that God is always uncomfortably near and He IS watching. Whilst He isn't the only one, He's the one that matters the most. What's more, God isn't interested in the outward impression you give, He sees beneath the surface – He examines your heart! Nothing goes unnoticed because He can watch the apples *and* the chocolate chip cookies!

PRAYER

All-seeing God, help me to live to please You and not to kid myself that there are things You don't notice. In Jesus' name. Amen.

BIBLE READING

No one who lives in Him keeps on sinning **1 John 3:1–10**
God sees what is done in secret **Matthew 6:16–18**

FURTHER REFLECTION

'Conscience is that inner voice which warns us someone may be looking.'

Henry Louis Mencken – American journalist, editor, critic and satirist (1880–1956)

Lord, You know what is best;
let this be done or that be done as You please.
Give what You will, as much as You will, when You will.
Do with me as You know best.
I am in Your hand; turn me about whichever way You will.
Behold, I am Your servant, ready to obey in all things.
Not for myself do I desire to live, but for You
– would that I could do this worthily and perfectly! Amen.

Thomas à Kempis – German monk and author of The Imitation of Christ *(1379–1471)*

SMILE

'A man breaks into a house at night. He is crossing a room when he hears a voice say, "Jesus and I can see you." He turns round and sees a parrot. Startled, he says, "You're a clever bird." "I know," came the reply. "What's your name?" asks the burglar. "Marmaduke," the parrot squawked. "That's a funny name to give a parrot." "Not as funny as giving the name 'Jesus' to a Rottweiler!"'

Anon.

37 STEPPING INTO OUR SHOES

We say some silly things sometimes. Such as, 'The kettle's boiling!' You may have already said it today. We don't actually mean the kettle's boiling; if it is, boy, we really are in trouble!

It often takes the questions of a young child to expose the weakness of some of our phrases, like the oft-quoted, 'I know how you feel'. Years ago, when my son was four years old and out shopping with his mum, he said, 'Mum, I wish you were me and I was you ... Because, if you was me, and I was you, then you'd know how much my tummy hurts!' The fact is we don't always know how another person is feeling. However sincerely we try, unless we've stood in another person's shoes, we can never tell if they're pinching.

So what about God? Can He ever tell how any human being feels? Well, I believe that God took a significant step to do so. When Jesus was born, it was as though God stepped into our shoes and lived among us. He didn't remain aloof from the problems of His world, but exposed Himself to life as we know it – with all its joy and pain.

MAYBE TODAY you don't have to wish that you were God and He were you. Simply remember and believe that God is with you and understands you.

PRAYER

Ever-loving God, however I'm feeling today, help me to know that You know me completely. Assure me of Your presence and grant me Your help and guidance. Make me mindful of the needs of others too, through Jesus Christ our Lord. Amen.

BIBLE READING

JESUS WEEPS **John 11:17–37**
THE WORD BECOMES FLESH **John 1:1–14**

FURTHER REFLECTION

Let earth and heaven combine,
Angels and men agree,
To praise in songs divine
The incarnate Deity,
Our God contracted to a span,
Incomprehensibly made man.

Charles Wesley – hymn-writer, poet, evangelist and co-founder of the Methodist movement with his brother, John (1707–1788)

SMILE

Picture the night before Christmas in a Methodist church – one well known to me!

Minister: 'Of course, we will need to be prepared, so that we have something to put in the crib after the Midnight Communion service. That way all will be complete for the children on Christmas morning.'

Church Steward: 'Oh dear. I have a confession. I have been looking for Jesus everywhere and I can't find him. What shall we do? He's gone missing.'

TM

38 FOOTPRINTS

A person first walked on the moon on 20 July 1969. Do you remember Neil Armstrong's words? 'That's one small step for (a) man, one giant leap for mankind.' There's no wind or atmosphere on the moon, so apparently the footprints of those who have landed on the moon are still there. It's remarkable to think that so many years later, there's evidence of moonwalks; the journey can be traced – the footsteps can still be seen!

I believe it was the astronaut James A. Lovell who said: 'God walking on the earth is more important than man walking on the moon.' Nevertheless, over 2,000 years on, the actual footprints of Jesus on the earth can't be seen in the sand of the Holy Land – you can only imagine Jesus walking there.

MAYBE TODAY people could see Jesus' footsteps in yours, if you seek to follow Him closely and obediently? For this you will need the wind of the Holy Spirit in your life and endeavour to maintain an atmosphere of love, forgiveness and peace around you.

PRAYER

Emmanuel (God with us), help me to tread boldly with You today. Amen.

BIBLE READING

A PRAYER FOR DIRECTION **Psalm 119:89–147**
THE RISEN JESUS SHOWS HIS HANDS AND FEET **Luke 24:36–53**

FURTHER REFLECTION

'A journey of a thousand miles starts with one step.'
Arab Proverb

When we walk with the Lord
In the light of his word,
What a glory he sheds on our way!
While we do his good will,
He abides with us still,
And with all who will trust and obey:

> *Trust and obey,*
> *for there's no other way*
> *To be happy in Jesus,*
> *But to trust and obey.*

John Henry Sammis – a businessman and YMCA worker who became an ordained
Presbyterian minister (1846–1919)

SMILE

'So I said to this train driver, "I want to go to Paris."
He said, "Eurostar?" I said, "I've been on telly, but I'm no
Dean Martin."'

Tim Vine – English stand-up comedian and actor (1967–)

39 HOLY POSSESSION

During the Second World War, the Dutch evangelist Corrie
ten Boom and her family hid Jewish refugees in their home
as Hitler's army invaded Holland. They were arrested, and
in her book *The Hiding Place*, Corrie wrote about life in the
Ravensbruck concentration camp. Amazingly she survived
to tell of God's love despite her experiences. She forgave her
captors and encouraged others to seek reconciliation.

This was only possible with the help of the Holy Spirit. Corrie
wrote, 'I have a glove here in my hand. The glove cannot do
anything by itself, but when my hand is in it, it can do many
things. True, it is not the glove, but my hand in the glove that
acts. We are gloves. It is the Holy Spirit in us who is the hand,
who does the job. We have to make room for the hand so that
every finger is filled.'[1]

The Nazis were seeking to control the world by evil means.
Corrie resisted by allowing God's Spirit to possess her instead:
her body became a temple for the Holy Spirit.

MAYBE TODAY you could remember the day of Pentecost.
After obediently waiting in Jerusalem, the believers were filled
with the Spirit. Wherever you are, whatever opposition or
persecution you may be facing, whatever challenges or obstacles
lie ahead, whatever your weaknesses or vulnerabilities, the
same Holy Spirit can transform you too. Simply open your
heart and pray that you may be filled with the essence and
power of Jesus.

PRAYER

*Enter the 'hiding place' of my heart, Lord. Possess me with Your
love and live within me by Your Spirit. Amen.*

BIBLE READING

THE DAY OF PENTECOST **Acts 2:1–13**
GOD'S TEMPLE **1 Corinthians 3:16–17**

FURTHER REFLECTION

O that the Comforter would come,
Nor visit as a transient guest,
But fix in me his constant home,
And take possession of my breast,
And fix in me his loved abode,
The temple of indwelling God!

Charles Wesley – hymn-writer, poet, evangelist and co-founder of the Methodist movement with his brother, John (1707–1788)

SMILE

'One of the first things that happens when a man is really filled with the Holy Spirit is not that he speaks in tongues, but that he learns to hold the one that he already has.'

J. Sidlow Baxter – pastor, theologian and author (1903–1999)

40 CARRIED TO JESUS

It was most likely a typical Palestinian house belonging to Simon Peter. Nothing more than a single room with an outside stairway onto a roof that was probably made up of wooden beams, overlaid with branches and covered with mud. This structure had to be repaired before the annual rainy season.

On this occasion the house was packed. Many had come to see Jesus, hear Him preach, and witness people being healed. Due to the crowds, four men carried a paralytic man onto the roof. They then made a hole in the covering and lowered him before Jesus. They must have been determined to get this man into Jesus' presence, for they didn't lose hope when they realised just what they had to do. Rather, using their energy and ingenuity, the friends sought Jesus' help. They believed that the Lord could meet the man's needs and they weren't going to give up. What a marvellous act of intercession! They literally brought someone into the presence of Jesus. Surely, this is what our prayers for others should be like. With our mind's eye, we should be bringing people to the Healer. It's this boldness, determination and trust that the writer of Mark's Gospel calls 'Faith'. In this story, it's even more important than fully understanding Jesus and His mission.

MAYBE TODAY you could identify those who need help, healing and forgiveness, and then carry them in your heart into Jesus' presence. This takes determined prayer and a trust in God's love. It's the faith of such 'carriers' that enables Jesus' gracious acts of healing, and His identification of people's real needs.

PRAYER

Saviour Jesus, I bring to You those I am concerned about today.
May they know Your healing presence; meet their deepest needs,
and answer my prayers as You know best. Amen.

BIBLE READING

JESUS HEALS A PARALYTIC **Mark 2:1–12**
JESUS' TEACHING ON PRAYER **Luke 11:1–13**

FURTHER REFLECTION

What a friend we have in Jesus,
All our sins and griefs to bear!
What a privilege to carry
Everything to God in prayer!
O what peace we often forfeit,
O what needless pain we bear,
All because we do not carry
Everything to God in prayer!

Joseph Medlicott Scriven – Irish philanthropist who embraced the teaching of the
Plymouth Brethren (1820–1886)

SMILE

Q: What did the paralysed man say to Jesus?
A: 'My friends have let me down.'

Anon.

Q: How many of the paralysed man's friends did it take to change the light bulb?
A: All four – one to change the light bulb and the other three to rebuild the ceiling first.

Anon.

41 ME AND MY GOD

Do you remember the song and dance, 'Me and My Shadow'? Frank Sinatra performed it with Sammy Davis Jr. I also know someone who's perfected it as an entertaining party-piece with his wife. The humour of the routine is in the shadow that appears to have a life of its own.

It's tempting to treat God like a shadow, because He's always there when needed for company or reassurance. 'Me and my friend *God*, strolling down the avenue!' I'm in control of *my* life, but God is there for me to fall back on.

But God is the life-giver! He doesn't follow me. Rather, I should follow His instruction, for He's the Master who is to be worshipped and obeyed. What's more, He's not *my* God alone, but the God of everyone: 'O LORD, *our* Lord …,' says the psalmist on more than one occasion (Psalm 8:1,9, my italics).

The book of Psalms is in the middle of the Bible and its chapters are among the most frequently thumbed pages. When I read them, I'm conscious I'm using what would have been Jesus' prayer or hymnbook! His spiritual life was nourished by a life of worship that included psalms.

MAYBE TODAY when, like Sinatra, you're 'all alone and feeling blue', turn not to a shadow, but to the light of God's Word. Then, perhaps, God will shine through you and so brighten the lives of others too, for He's *our* Lord, not yours alone!

PRAYER

O Lord, our Lord, lead me out of darkness into Your marvellous light, that I may be Yours in obedience. Amen.

BIBLE READING

JESUS COMES TO THOSE IN DARKNESS **Matthew 4:12–17**
THE LIGHT OF THE KNOWLEDGE OF THE GLORY OF GOD
2 Corinthians 4:1–12

FURTHER REFLECTION

Grant, O Lord, that the light of your love may never be dimmed within us.
Let it shine forth from our warmed hearts to comfort others
in times of peace and in seasons of adversity,
and in bright beams of your goodness and love
may we come at last to the vision of your glory;
through Christ our Lord. Amen.

St Columbanus – Irish abbot and missionary (550–615)

SMILE

It always amuses me when people choose to have 'My Way' by Frank Sinatra played at the crematorium. I can't be the only person who finds the lyrics amusing: 'And now, the end is near; and so I face the final curtain.'

TM

42 EXCUSES

One morning my wife informed me that she was going to the hairdresser. Our paths parted and, as the day progressed, it proved to be a stressful one. Later, Frances and I were reunited at home. I poured out my woes to my soul mate. Whilst listening, Frances looked at me intently, obviously wanting something. I promptly started to help make the dinner, but my lack of assistance wasn't the issue. 'You haven't noticed my hair!' she said despairingly. Woops! I tried to blame poor light, my bad memory and my preoccupation with the day's troubles. Nevertheless, I was without excuse, especially as I had been pre-warned! The expensive hairdo was stunning and evident to all with eyes to see.

Paul wrote, 'For since the creation of the world God's invisible qualities – his eternal power and divine nature – have been clearly seen … so that men are without excuse' (Romans 1:20). The ungodly deserve to be punished for not responding to God's revealed truth. Why? Well, they're without excuse because it was made plain to them. Since creation, God's invisible qualities have been clearly revealed in His handiwork, power and nature. Those who deny God's existence reap the consequences for their wilful rebellion. However, just as Frances forgave me, God will pardon those who turn to Him, open their eyes and admit their neglect.

MAYBE TODAY you should ask, 'What have I done with my knowledge of God?'

PRAYER

Creator God, shine the light of Your beautiful nature into the darkness of my preoccupied mind, that I may see Your truth. Amen.

BIBLE READING

GOD'S WRATH **Romans 1:18–32**

IN GOD WE LIVE AND HAVE OUR BEING **Acts 17:24–28**

FURTHER REFLECTION

What shall I give you, Lord, in return for all your kindness?

Glory to you for your love.

Glory to you for your patience.

Glory to you for forgiving us all our sins.

Glory to you for coming to save our souls.

Glory to you for your incarnation in the virgin's womb.

Glory to you for your bonds.

Glory to you for receiving the cut of the lash.

Glory to you for accepting mockery.

Glory to you for your crucifixion.

Glory to you for your burial.

Glory to you for your resurrection.

Glory to you that you were preached to all.

Glory to you in whom they believed.

Ephrem the Syrian – prolific Syriac-language poet and theologian (306–373)

SMILE

'A flimsy excuse is one your wife can see through.'

Anon.

LISTEN, LISTEN! I AM FOR YOU

Listen, Listen! I am for you – I will never let you go.

Sorry, haven't got the time – we're too busy – busy
struggling:
>   To keep the wolf from the door
>   To keep our heads above water
>   To keep the kids happy
>   To keep the peace
>   To keep the job
>   To keep up with the Joneses
>   To just keep going.

Listen, Listen! You need to keep your stress levels down
a bit – didn't you hear what I said? I am for you – I will
never let you go. I know how tough it is – and I can't
magic the toughness away – but, with me beside you,
within you, we can work together – let me take the
strain. I am your Father, your Mother – my love for you
will never end.

Can we talk another time? Right now we're fighting a
losing battle:
>   Against the belly full of hunger
>   Against the hate that pulls the trigger
>   Against the mutant virus
>   Against the lies and the spin
>   Against the wealth never shared
>   Against the darkness and the pain
>   Against … everything!

Listen, Listen! Every pain you feel – I too have felt. Every crushing blow – I too have known. Every set back – I too have experienced. Remember the cross? Hold on to me – for the struggle in the dark *will* give way to the sunrise and the peace of a new day; the flood tide of hurt and pain *will* ebb away and bring healing. I have overcome. Remember the empty tomb? I am your Brother and I'm with you all the way.

Have you got a minute God? We can't seem to do this on our own; we make a mess, then we try to put it right and the mess multiplies, like rabbits. It's hopeless!

Listen, Listen! There'll always be a mess – that's what children do – and you are my children. But hopeless? Never! For every day I am sweeping away injustice – take time to look and you will see this. Every day I am rebuilding broken hearts – this will be revealed to you. Every day, someone is set free – you will know it when you see it.

But I just need more willing hearts and hands, fertile imaginations, skills – which you have in abundance, for I have given them to you. I need you to follow my lead and little by little, we will make a difference.

Is that a promise Lord?

I am your Soul-friend – and I would not lie to you.

PRAYER AND PRAISE

43 PROMISES, PROMISES

I often find myself promising to pray for people – it's an occupational hazard! I do it, not because it's my job, but because I care and genuinely want to express pastoral concern and my trust in a loving God, our Helper and Healer, who I believe can make a difference. Many things are possible through our own human effort, but made powerful through prayer.

The trouble is, well-intentioned promises can simply be forgotten after they have flowed easily from our lips. Busy lives and overloaded memories are often to blame. If you're honest, at some time I'm sure you've said 'I'll pray for you' and then felt guilty afterwards because you didn't.

Like a good *Method*ist, I now have a 'method' to help me to keep my promises. I have a prayer journal to remind me what to pray for and when. My system consists of a mixture of handwritten notes, my diary and a handy computer programme. All I have to remember is to write down or input what I've promised before my 'memory of a goldfish' kicks in.

MAYBE TODAY is a day for ensuring you pray for those in need and are faithful to your word. Don't be embarrassed by having to write things down or recording them electronically. My experience is that, although you may be teased for being so organised, you will also be respected and encouraged by those who realise you take prayer seriously and that your promises are more than mere pious platitudes.

PRAYER

Lord, You taught us how to pray and showed us that the needs of individuals matter. Grant me a big heart, a healthy methodical prayer life, and every confidence that Your grace and mercy can make all the difference. Amen.

BIBLE READING

PRAY FOR EACH OTHER **James 5:13–20**
LIFT UP HOLY HANDS IN PRAYER **1 Timothy 2:1–8**

FURTHER REFLECTION

'If you pray for another, you will be helped yourself.'
A Jewish proverb

When God inclines the heart to pray
He hath an ear to hear;
To him there's music in a groan
And beauty in a tear.
The humble seeker cannot fail,
To have his needs supplied,
Since He for sinners intercedes,
Who once for sinners died.

Benjamin Beddome – Baptist preacher and hymn-writer (1717–1795)

SMILE

'Vicar, will you pray for my floating kidneys?'
Vicar: 'I don't pray for specific complaints.'
'But you did last week, you prayed for loose livers.'[1]

44 GOD'S HEARTBEAT

After a busy day I went to bed exhausted. I couldn't sleep,
however, because so many things were racing through my
mind. The more I tried to doze off, the harder it became.
The last thing I remember, as my head lay on the pillow, was
hearing my heart beating steadily. In the morning, I was
reminded of a saying from a monk of Patmos: 'Those who lean
on Jesus' breast hear God's heartbeat.'

According to tradition, John was 'the disciple Jesus loved'
and he was exiled on the Isle of Patmos, where he eventually
died. In John's Gospel, we read that he reclined against Jesus at
the Last Supper (John 13:23f). Hence the monk's words about
leaning on 'Jesus' breast'. I'm often 'worried and upset about
many things', and forget that to keep close to Jesus is all that is
needed (Luke 10:38f).

MAYBE TODAY, despite life's pressures, is a day for leaning
closer to Jesus; for letting the reality of God's ever-present love
soothe your soul with peace. Perhaps this is what is needed to
revive you as a servant of the Lord. What's more, it may help
you to pray the words of the songwriter, Graham Kendrick,
'Teach me to dance to the beat of your heart'.

PRAYER

Almighty God, help me to keep close to Jesus,
especially through my prayer and devotions.
May I lean upon my Lord and listen.
Help me to hear His heartbeat
and live confidently knowing that He is my Living Saviour.
Guide me that I might live a way that is in harmony with Your
Holy Spirit
and NOT dance to the world's tune.
Rather, release me to discover Your holy rhythm of life.

Then, as I let the Lord of the dance lead me,
may my steps take me through the difficult places
to the place of Your glory, peace and eternal joy.
I ask this in the name of my companion and Lord. Amen.

BIBLE READING

HE GATHERS THE LAMBS **Isaiah 40:11**
MOURNING TURNED TO DANCING **Jeremiah 31:16–34**

FURTHER REFLECTION

I heard the voice of Jesus say:
'Come unto me and rest;
Lay down, thou weary one, lay down
Thy head upon my breast.'
I came to Jesus as I was,
Weary and worn and sad,
I found in him a resting-place,
And he has made me glad.

Horatius Bonar – Scottish Presbyterian minister and hymn-writer (1808–1889)

SMILE
'She does a dance suggesting the life of a fern; I saw one
of the rehearsals, and to me it could have equally well
suggested the life of John Wesley.'

Saki (Hector Hugh Munro) – novelist and short story writer (1870–1916)

45 FIND YOUR MOUNTAIN

I find it makes a difference when I fall to my knees. Why? Well, 'prayer changes things'. Some will argue that answers to prayer are merely coincidences. Yet, isn't it strange that when Christians stop praying 'coincidences' stop happening? It's also true to say that prayer doesn't always change 'things', but often 'people', then it's those 'people' who change 'things'!

Jesus never took a step without His Father's approval. One example is when He was about to head towards Jerusalem and the cross. About eight days after Peter had confessed that Jesus was 'The Christ of God', we read that '… [Jesus] took Peter, John and James with him and went up onto a mountain to pray' (Luke 9:28). He went to pray with His friends.

Traditionally, it's thought they went up Mount Tabor, but it could have been the solitude of Mount Hermon. It's as Christ prayerfully humbles Himself that a mysterious 'transfiguration' takes place. No doubt Jesus had thought very hard about whether He was doing the right thing in heading for Jerusalem. But, by taking 'time out' upon the mountain, He is exalted: a change takes place, and God stamps His divine seal of approval upon the decision to give His life to save the world.

MAYBE TODAY, whatever uncertainties or challenges lie ahead, you could make time to pray – alone, or with friends. But this comes with a warning: expect the unexpected, and be prepared for change!

PRAYER

Lord Jesus, help me find my 'mountain' today and may I know Your transforming power. Amen.

BIBLE READING

JESUS PRAYS BEFORE CHOOSING HIS DISCIPLES **Luke 6:12–16**
MOSES ON THE MOUNTAIN **Exodus 24:12–18**

FURTHER REFLECTION

Lord Jesus, our Saviour, let us now come to you:
Our hearts are cold; Lord, warm them with your selfless love.
Our hearts are sinful; cleanse them with your precious blood.
Our hearts are weak; strengthen them with your joyous Spirit.
Our hearts are empty; fill them with your divine presence.
Lord Jesus, our hearts are yours; possess them always and only
for yourself. Amen.

*St Augustine of Hippo – influential Christian thinker, philosopher/theologian
(354–430)*

SMILE

'Apparently there is even a 'Dial A Prayer' service for
Atheists – you dial a number and no one answers!'

Anon.

46 BUSINESS AND PRAYER

Brother Lawrence was a monk in the seventeenth century. He is usually remembered for his close relationship with God. His book *The Practice of the Presence of God* is a Christian classic. Lawrence developed his rule of spirituality and work when working in the monastery kitchen. He once said, 'The time of business does not with me differ from the time of prayer; and in the noise and clatter of my kitchen, while several persons are at the same time calling for different things, I possess God in as great tranquility as if I were upon my knees at the blessed sacrament'.[2]

It's my experience that some Christians unconsciously segregate different areas of their lives. Going to church is a 'holy' thing to do and we expect to find God there; whereas the mundane and tedious side of life's routine isn't treated the same. Brother Lawrence challenged this attitude with the conviction that God's love could be known and experienced in any 'common business'. The important thing isn't the sacredness, or worldly status, of what we do, but what it is that motivates us. He said, 'We can do *little* things for God; I turn the cake that is frying on the pan for the love of Him, and that done, if there is nothing else to call me, I prostrate myself in worship before Him, who has given me grace to work; afterwards I rise happier than a king. It is enough for me to pick up but a straw from the ground for the love of God'.[3]

MAYBE TODAY is a day for finding God in the ordinary and unexpected places – even the kitchen!

PRAYER

Forgive me, Lord, for not living the whole of my life for You, and with You. Amen.

BIBLE READING

A MIRACLE IN THE KITCHEN **1 Kings 17:7–16**
SERVE WHOLEHEARTEDLY **Ephesians 6:5–9**

FURTHER REFLECTION

'O my God, since Thou art with me,
and I must now, in obedience to Thy commands,
apply my mind to these outward things,
I beseech Thee to grant me the grace to continue in Thy presence;
and to this end do Thou prosper me with Thy assistance,
receive all my works, and possess all my affections.'[4]

'Lord of all pots and pans and things …
Make me a saint by getting meals
And washing up the plates!'[5]

Brother Lawrence – Carmelite monk (1605–1691)

SMILE

'An efficiency expert concluded his lecture with a note of caution. "You need to be careful about trying these techniques at home." "Why?" asked somebody from the audience. "I watched my wife's routine at dinner for years," the expert explained. "She made lots of trips between the refrigerator, stove, table and cabinets, often carrying a single item at a time. One day I told her, 'Honey, why don't you try carrying several things at once?'" "Did it save time?" the guy in the audience asked. "Actually, yes," replied the expert. "It used to take her thirty minutes to make dinner. Now I do it in ten …"'

Anon.

47 PRAYING IN THE GAP

I used to visit an elderly housebound lady, who spent her days in an armchair. On one armrest was her Bible, and on the other, a newspaper. Each day she'd faithfully read the Scriptures and then pray through the paper. She longed to see a national spiritual revival and social change. There's much she couldn't do, but 'I'm blessed with time to pray,' she'd say with a smile. 'I prayerfully sit *in the gap* between the world and heaven.' A lovely image!

In Psalm 85 we read, 'Restore us again, O God our Saviour … Will you prolong your anger through all generations?' (Psa. 85:4–5). At the beginning of the psalm the psalmist remembered how God had restored His people in the past. Now he prays for the present. The nation had previously experienced mercy and deliverance, but now God (who can't stand godlessness) was angry at their behaviour again. Their only hope was God's mercy; that He would save and purify them once and for all. The psalmist prays that their wrongdoing may be set aside, so that God's righteous indignation would be pacified.

These verses ultimately find their fulfilment in the New Testament. Jesus is the only hope for individuals and the nations today. He stood 'in the gap' for us upon the cross. His death and resurrection made forgiveness possible for all who'll turn towards Him with faith.

MAYBE TODAY you could pray for this nation, our government and prime minister with a Bible in one hand and newspaper in the other. For whatever you think of those in power, our ultimate hope is in the holy and merciful Lord Jesus.

PRAYER

Restoring God, thank You for uniting heaven and earth through Jesus, and for giving hope to all generations. Amen.

BIBLE READING

RESTORE US AGAIN **Psalm 85**
PHILIP AND THE ETHIOPIAN **Acts 8:26–40**

FURTHER REFLECTION

I knelt to pray but not for long, I had too much to do,
Must hurry up and get to work, for bills would soon be due.
And so I said a hurried prayer, jumped up from off my knees,
My Christian duty now was done, my soul could be at ease.
All through the day I had no time to speak a word of cheer,
No time to speak to those in need; they'd laugh at me, I feared.
No time, no time – too much to do, that was my constant cry,
No time to give to those in need. At last 'twas time to die.
And when before the Lord I came, I stood with downcast eyes.
Within his hands he held a book. It was the book of life.
God looked into his book and said, 'Your name I cannot find,
I once was going to write it down, but never found the time.'
Anon.

SMILE

'Prayerlessness is a sin.'
Corrie ten Boom – a Dutch Christian Holocaust survivor and evangelist (1892–1983)

48 SHARPENING UP

Whenever work seems to overtake me, I recall a folk tale about two woodmen. They set about chopping logs for a whole day. It was exhausting work. One chopped constantly without a break, but the other chilled for at least ten minutes in each hour. Despite his resting, it was the second woodman that chopped the most wood.

The first man was frustrated and confused by this. He'd worked so hard, but had achieved less. He asked if his workmate would share his secret of success. 'It's quite simple,' his friend said, 'whenever I rested, I sharpened my axe.'

MAYBE TODAY it's time to build time-out into your schedule. Even Jesus took a break from time to time to recharge His batteries physically and spiritually, and He had the whole world to save. What's more, we should remember that the Bible tells us that after six days of creation, God rested. You will be sharper and more at one with God's rhythm of life if you put your feet up on a regular basis.

PRAYER

God of the Sabbath, teach me to rest and not feel guilty; to reflect and find renewal, in Jesus' name. Amen.

BIBLE READING

Elijah flees to Horeb **1 Kings 19:1–9**
Ten Commandments **Deuteronomy 5:1–22**

FURTHER REFLECTION

Come now, turn aside for a while from your daily employment,
escape for a moment from the tumult of your thoughts.
Put aside your weighty cares,
let your burdensome distractions wait,
free yourself for a while for God
and rest awhile in him.
Enter the inner chamber of your soul,
shut out everything except God
and that which can help you in seeking him,
and when you have shut the door, seek him.
Now, my soul, say to God,
'I seek your face; Lord it is your face that I seek.' Amen.

St Anselm of Canterbury – Italian clergyman, scholastic philosopher and theologian (1033–1109)

SMILE

A student's exam paper:
Q. Can you list all of the Ten Commandments in any order?
A. 7,3,6,8,4,1,5,10,2,9.

Anon.

49 WORSHIP

One Sunday my wife couldn't go to church because of a journey she had to make. Whilst driving, Frances saw the most magnificent winter sunset. There and then her heart spontaneously responded in worship. She wondered how many others on the motorway were praising their Creator. Sadness washed over her as she guessed that, in their hurry, most wouldn't even notice the splendour of the evening sky, let alone acknowledge the One who made it.

In the beginning we were made to know God, but many have turned away from the truth, rejected Him, and their hearts have darkened. Paul wrote, 'For although they knew God, they neither glorified him as God nor gave thanks to him …' (Rom. 1:21). Though God has made Himself known, few worship Him; most live independently and egotistically. (*Ego*: 'Edging God Out'.) This lack of adoration isn't surprising, for unless we respond to His truth and give something back, we can't glorify Him.

MAYBE TODAY is a time for slowing down, acknowledging your Maker and offering your response. In the nineteenth century Archbishop William Temple wrote, 'To worship is to quicken the conscience by the holiness of God, to feed the mind with the truth of God, to purge the imagination by the beauty of God, to open the heart to the love of God, to devote the will to the purpose of God.'

PRAYER

When everything revolves around me and I don't honour You, Father, forgive me in Jesus' name. Amen.

BIBLE READING

THE CREATOR OF ALL THINGS IS WORSHIPPED **Revelation 4**
SING AND MAKE MUSIC IN YOUR HEART **Ephesians 5:15–21**

FURTHER REFLECTION

O worship the Lord in the beauty of holiness,
Bow down before him, his glory proclaim:
With gold of obedience and incense of lowliness,
Kneel and adore him: the Lord is his name.

John S.B. Monsell – Irish Anglican clergyman, poet and hymn-writer (1811–1875)

SMILE

Some go to church to take a walk;
Some go to church to laugh and talk;
Some go there to meet a friend;
Some go there their time to spend;
Some go there to meet a lover;
Some go there a fault to cover;
Some go there for speculation;
Some go there for observation;
Some go there to doze and nod;
The wise go there to worship God!

C.H. Spurgeon, British Reformed Baptist, called the 'Prince of Preachers', and a prolific writer (1834–1892)

MEETING GOD

She knew about Jesus.
When she fought her brother,
threw her clothes on the floor,
her mother had cried: *Jesus wept!*

She knew about God.
When she pinched her father's
last cigarette he shouted:
God knows, I'll get you!

She knew about Christmas.
She'd been an angel
with tinsel halo and wings
in a Nativity Play.

She knew about Easter.
She loved chocolate eggs
and the four day holiday
from office work.

She'd once held a Bible
as she stood in the dock,
swore to *tell the truth,
so help me God.*

But now it was different.
A voice was whispering
from the hollow inside her:
Child, you don't know me.

Who put the voice there?
Who made her listen?
It was God who spoke.
Her friend made her listen

so now she knows Jesus,
and talks often with God
as she and her friend
read the Bible together.

Kaye Lee
Copyright © Kaye Lee 2008. Used with permission.

LEARNING TO LIVE GOD'S WAY

50 GOD'S WAY

The Reverend Chun-Ming Kao was a former general secretary of the Presbyterian Church in Taiwan. He stood for human rights and democracy in that country. Now retired, he's been described as 'the pride of Taiwan' and 'the Apostle Paul of the twentieth century'. On 24 April 1980, Kao was arrested and imprisoned for more than four years. This was for offering asylum to a most-wanted political dissident under the Kuomintang regime. Whilst in prison, Kao wrote a poem on 27 June 1982. His words were entitled 'God's way' and this is the English translation:

> I asked the Lord for a bunch of fresh flowers
> but instead he gave me an ugly cactus
> with many thorns.
> I asked the Lord for some beautiful butterflies
> but instead he gave me many ugly
> and dreadful worms.
> I was threatened,
> I was disappointed.
> I mourned.
> But after many days,
> suddenly,
> I saw the cactus bloom
> with many beautiful flowers.
> And those worms
> became beautiful butterflies
> flying in the Spring wind.
> God's way is the best way.

Used by kind permission of Reverend Chun-Ming Kao.

MAYBE TODAY is a day for trusting the Lord, despite our confusions and lack of understanding. Could we, with John Wesley, dare to believe the best is yet to come?

PRAYER

Lord, whatever I face today, grant me patience and faith. In time may I see Your promises fulfilled in my life, in Jesus' name. Amen.

BIBLE READING

BLESSED IS THE ONE WHO TRUSTS IN THE LORD
Jeremiah 17:7–8
MORE THAN CONQUERORS **Romans 8:28–39**

FURTHER REFLECTION

These words were said to be repeated by John Wesley two or three times just before he died: 'Best of all is, God is with us.'

In his Preface to *Standard Sermons*, John also wrote:
'God himself has condescended to teach the way: for this very end he came from heaven. He hath written it down in a book. O give me that book! At any price give me the Book of God!'

John Wesley – Anglican clergyman, evangelist, and co-founder of the Methodist movement with his brother, Charles (1703–1791)

SMILE
'I can cope with despair: it's hope I can't take.'
From the 1986 comedy film Clockwise, starring John Cleese

51 PIN YOUR EARS BACK

Someone once said, 'God knew what He was doing when He gave us two ears and only one mouth' – so that we would do more listening than talking. Perhaps that's why He made the ears to remain open and the mouth to close!

MAYBE TODAY could be a day for endeavouring to say less, and for paying more attention to what others are saying to you? For if you truly listen, it will help you respond more appropriately to what you hear. This may also apply to your prayers, in case you miss what God is longing to communicate to your restless soul.

I recall the third verse of a hymn I used to enjoy singing at school, 'O Jesus, I have promised':

> O let me hear thee speaking
> In accents clear and still,
> Above the storms of passion,
> The murmurs of self-will;
> O speak to reassure me,
> To hasten or control;
> O speak, and make me listen,
> Thou guardian of my soul.
>
> *J.E. Bode 1816–1874*

PRAYER

Living God, help me to bite my tongue today and to keep my ears open, for Jesus' sake. Amen.

BIBLE READING

LISTENING AND DOING **James 1:19–27**
LISTENING TO GOD **Proverbs 8:32–35**

FURTHER REFLECTION

'Waiting upon God is not idleness, but work which beats all other work to one unskilled in it.'
'Hearing is a step towards vision.'

St Bernard of Clairvaux – French Cistercian abbot and mystic (1090–1153)

SMILE

'Better to keep your mouth shut and appear stupid than to open it and remove all doubt.'

Attributed to Mark Twain – pen name of Samuel Longhorne Clemens, American writer and satirist (1835–1910)

52 ALTERNATIVELY

Tragically, a lovely Christian lady was terminally ill with cancer. Despite the trial she had to endure, she possessed a tremendous attitude. One of her favourite quotes was, 'Two men look through prison bars; one sees mud, the other sees stars.'

She had a realistic and honest faith, but it enabled her to see God at work – even in the mundane. She was a fine example of someone who graciously saw the good in people, and who held on to the hope her beliefs gave her. She chose to look for, and indeed celebrate, the positives in every situation, rather than giving in to depression or despair. Each time I made a pastoral visit to her, I would come away feeling better! By always looking to God for strength and inspiration, she became like a light shining in the darkness. When she died there were many tears, but we celebrated her faith and life with hope and confidence.

MAYBE TODAY is a day for asking God to help us see our cup as being half full, rather than half empty. Honesty is important, but could it be that we sometimes choose not to look on the bright side of life because it suits us better?

PRAYER

God of love and hope, I give thanks that You see my potential and not just my faults. Help me to look to the stars rather than the mud, for I ask in the name of Jesus, my Saviour. Amen.

BIBLE READING

CHOOSE LIFE **Deuteronomy 30:11–20**
STAND AT THE CROSSROADS AND LOOK **Jeremiah 6:1–17**

FURTHER REFLECTION

'I believe we are solely responsible for our choices, and we have to accept the consequences of every deed, word and thought throughout our lifetime.'

Elisabeth Kübler-Ross – Swiss-born American psychiatrist (1926–2004)

SMILE

'Both optimists and pessimists contribute to society. The optimist invents the aeroplane, the pessimist the parachute.'

George Bernard Shaw – Irish-born playwright, social critic, essayist and political thinker (1856–1950)

53 IT'S MORE THAN BEING 'BRITISH'

Whatever happened to common courtesy or good manners? Like waiting for people to get off the bus or train before trying to get on? Or giving up one's seat for a pregnant woman or someone of more advanced years? Or in your car giving way to a funeral cortège? Or even simply letting a newcomer sit in one's seat in church without any resentment?

MAYBE TODAY is a day for being indecently decent through spontaneous generosity, as opposed to selfishly exercising your rights; or for being outrageously polite as a witness to your faith. Jesus set an example of showing great regard for others: the Son of God, gave up more than His seat – even His very life upon the cross, for love of those who didn't even deserve it!

PRAYER

Lord Jesus, help me to remember today that You said '… the last will be first, and the first will be last' (Matt. 20:16). Amen.

BIBLE READING

THE LAST WILL BE FIRST **Matthew 19:30–20:16**
WITH THE FIRST AND THE LAST **Isaiah 41:1–10**

FURTHER REFLECTION

Lord, teach me to be generous.
Teach me to serve you as you deserve;
to give and not to count the cost,
to fight and not to heed the wounds,
to toil and not to seek for rest,
to labour and not to ask for reward,
save that of knowing that I do your will. Amen.

St Ignatius of Loyola – Spanish founder of the Jesuits (1491–1556)

SMILE

'Children are natural mimics who act like their parents despite every effort to teach them good manners.'

Anon.

'The hardest job kids face today is learning good manners without seeing any.'

Attributed to Fred Astaire – dancer and actor (1899–1997)

54 ENCOURAGEMENT

The world can be a negative place. The tendency for the media to indulge in character assassination is an example. Another is the critical spirit that can creep into personal relationships, through gossip, selfishness and unrealistic expectations. Whatever happened to 'encouragement'? My wife, Frances, has a good definition of this characteristic. She says, 'It's the warm sun on a flower bud that helps it to blossom.'

True encouragement isn't empty praise or flattery. It isn't insincere glib statements, or a smarmy charm; it's not taking people for granted! Real encouragement is an expression of genuine appreciation and loving interest. It may be coming alongside someone, lifting their spirit and enabling them to flower. Sometimes it's just two little words, like 'thank you', or 'well done'. George M. Adams once said, 'Encouragement is oxygen to the soul.' In the Bible, Barnabas was called 'The son of encouragement'. He urged the apostles to embrace Paul and opened a way for him to develop a mission to the Gentiles in Antioch.

MAYBE TODAY you could be a 'Barnabas'. Someone once said, 'The church should be a community of encouragement'.

PRAYER

Transforming Lord, may my faith become the 'darkroom' that turns all my 'negatives' to 'positives'. Amen.

BIBLE READING

PAUL AND BARNABAS ENCOURAGE THE DISCIPLES
Acts 14:21–25
A STRONG MESSAGE **Isaiah 1:16b–18**

FURTHER REFLECTION

All praise to our redeeming Lord,
Who joins us by his grace,
And bids us, each to each restored,
Together seek his face.

He bids us build each other up;
And, gathered into one,
To our high calling's glorious hope
We hand in hand go on.

And if our fellowship below
In Jesus be so sweet,
What heights of rapture shall we know
When round his throne we meet!

Charles Wesley – hymn-writer, poet, evangelist and co-founder of the Methodist movement with his brother, John (1707–1788)

SMILE
'Honest criticism is hard to take, especially from a relative, a friend, an acquaintance, or a stranger.'

Franklin P. Jones – businessman and humorist (1887–1929)

55 WISDOM

I once interviewed Olive Morgan, a wise Christian lady who'd taken up blogging in her eighties! She's a fascinating and amusing person and many young people are interested in what she has to say on the internet. Surely, this generation needs the wisdom that mature, prayerful and experienced Christians like Olive can offer.

Wisdom is frequently referred to in the Bible. I think it's a quality that's possessed through an understanding of ourselves, others and God.

Firstly, *ourselves*: the preacher, Charles Haddon Spurgeon, suggested, 'The door step to wisdom is a knowledge of your own ignorance.' Secondly, *others*: Abraham Lincoln said, 'When I'm getting ready to reason with a man I spend one-third of my time thinking about myself and what I am going to say – and two-thirds thinking about him and what he is going to say.'

Thirdly, and most importantly, GOD: Billy Graham once said, 'Knowledge is horizontal; wisdom is vertical and comes from above.' Hence the psalmist wrote, 'The fear of the LORD is the beginning of wisdom; all who follow his precepts have good understanding. To him belongs eternal praise' (Psa. 111:10).

MAYBE TODAY is a day for praying for wisdom in all you are doing or facing at this time.

PRAYER

*God grant me the serenity to accept the things I cannot change,
the courage to change the things I can,
and the wisdom to distinguish one from the other.*

Reinhold Niebuhr – American theologian (1892–1971)

BIBLE READING

THE FEAR OF THE LORD IS THE BEGINNING OF WISDOM
Psalm 111
WISE AND FOOLISH BUILDERS **Luke 6:46–49**

FURTHER REFLECTION

Wisdom is the finest beauty of a person.
Money does not prevent you from becoming blind.
Money does not prevent you from becoming mad.
Money does not prevent you from becoming lame.
You may be ill in any part of your body, so it is
better for you to go and think again
and to select wisdom.
Come and sacrifice, that you may have rest in your body,
inside and outside.

Traditional African prayer [1]

SMILE

'If you want people to think you are wise,
just agree with them.'

Leo Calvin Rosten – teacher, academic and humorist (1908–1997)

56 SLEEPWALKING

My daughter used to sleepwalk when she was a child. It was disconcerting to see Hannah climb downstairs with her eyes wide open, knowing she was asleep. She gave every impression of being awake, but the reality was quite different. Gently, we'd persuade her to go back to bed – which was difficult enough when she was awake!

Sometimes, adults too can give the appearance of being awake when actually we're 'spiritually sleepwalking'. The joys and trials of life make people weary, both physically and faith-wise too.

It happened to the disciples – Peter, James and John. They were sleepy at the time of Jesus' transfiguration. Luke 9:32 reveals that, 'Peter and his companions were very sleepy …' It wasn't until they were fully awake that they '… saw his glory and the two men standing with him'.

The disciples were exhausted again in the garden of Gethsemane before Jesus' crucifixion.

We can also become drowsy in heart and mind and fail to reflect on our experiences; fail to wrestle with our consciences; fail to hear what our Lord is saying to us; or fail to see the glorious new thing that God wants to do in our lives or the world at large. Are we sleepwalking, for example, whilst an estimated 40 million people are living with HIV/AIDS and nearly three million are dying each year?

MAYBE TODAY you could check you are *fully awake*, for the philosopher, Plato, said 'The unexamined life is not worth living'.

PRAYER

Lord, don't let the rhythm of life rock me into a slumber. Rather, keep me conscious of Your purposes and glory. Amen.

BIBLE READING
THE TRANSFIGURATION **Luke 9:28–36**
THE PARABLE OF THE TEN VIRGINS **Matthew 25:1–13**

FURTHER REFLECTION
God of miracles and wonders,
shatter our complacency;
challenge our apathy;
feed our spiritual curiosity;
until our restless souls
find peace in Your grace and mercy.
This we pray, in the name of our Saviour, Jesus,
who came that we might find spiritual freedom
and everlasting life. Amen.

TM

SMILE
Q. Are you a light sleeper?
A. No, I sleep in the dark.

Q. Doctor, I snore so loud that I keep myself awake.
A. Sleep in another room then!

Anon.

A FUTURE NOT OF OUR OWN

It helps, now and then, to step back
and take the long view.
The kingdom is not only beyond our efforts,
it is beyond our vision.
We accomplish in our lifetime only a tiny fraction of
the magnificent enterprise that is God's work.
Nothing we do is complete,
which is another way of saying
that the kingdom always lies beyond us.
No statement says all that could be said.
No prayer fully expresses our faith.
No confession brings perfection.
No pastoral visit brings wholeness.
No program accomplishes the church's mission.
No set of goals and objectives includes everything.
This is what we are about:
We plant seeds that one day will grow.
We water seeds already planted,
knowing that they hold future promise.
We lay foundations that will need further development.
We provide yeast that produces effects beyond our
capabilities.
We cannot do everything
and there is a sense of liberation in realizing that.
This enables us to do something,
and to do it very well.
It may be incomplete, but it is a beginning,
a step along the way,
an opportunity for God's grace to enter and do the rest.

We may never see the end results,
but that is the difference between the master builder
and the worker.
We are workers, not master builders,
ministers, not messiahs.
We are prophets of a future not our own.

Attributed to Oscar Romero – Latin American Archbishop (1917–1980)

SEASONS

57 YOU

In the midst of the last minute panic to get ready for Christmas, my wife, Frances, was ploughing through a pile of Christmas cards, envelopes and stamps. It was late in the evening and she was very tired, clearly wanting to conclude the annual ritual. Suddenly, the words from a card leapt out at her: 'Today in the town of David a Saviour has been born to *YOU* …' (Luke 2:11). Jesus wasn't merely Mary's baby, or Joseph's – the angel made it clear that Christ was born for the shepherds, for the magi, for YOU and me! What an amazingly obvious and profound truth. It's for YOU a child is born!

MAYBE TODAY I ought to ponder this great truth: That God so loved the world … and so loved me … that He sent His only Son to be MY Saviour.

PRAYER

Lord, despite the busyness and pressure of the day, be born anew in my heart, that I may know You as MY Saviour … always … and long for others to know You as their Saviour too! Amen.

BIBLE READING

THE SHEPHERDS AND THE ANGELS **Luke 2:8–20**
JESUS TEACHES NICODEMUS **John 3:1–21**

FURTHER REFLECTION

'Blessed art thou O Christmas Christ, that thy cradle was so low that shepherds, poorest and simplest of earthly folk, could yet kneel beside it … and look level-eyed into the face of God.'
Anon.

SMILE

Three men died on Christmas Eve and were met by Saint Peter at the Pearly Gates. 'In honour of this holy season,' Saint Peter said, 'you must each possess something that symbolizes Christmas in order to get into heaven.'

The first man fumbled through his pockets and pulled out a lighter. He flicked it on. 'It represents a candle,' he said. 'You may pass through the pearly gates,' said Saint Peter.

The second man reached into his pocket and pulled out a set of keys. He shook them and said, 'They're bells.' Peter said, 'You may pass through the pearly gates.'

The third man started searching desperately through his pockets and finally pulled out a pair of women's tights. Saint Peter looked at the man with a raised eyebrow and asked, 'And just what do those symbolise?' The man replied, 'These are Carol's!'

Anon.

58 WHOSE CHRISTMAS?

Are you any good at anagrams? Try re-arranging the letters of the following three words to see if you can find the two words you think I am looking for: IT'S ONLY ME. The answer is revealed below.*

How did you get on? A further anagram of the answer is IT'S MY NOEL.

Both anagrams are about me. There's a danger that my life can revolve around Tony Miles too. Take *It's my Noel*, for example: If I plan Christmas around what *I* want, then *I* will be, inevitably and selfishly, at the centre of everything. Obviously, looking after self is important, especially spiritually, physically and emotionally. Yet, the words 'sin' and 'pride' both have 'I' at the centre of them. Someone once said, 'It's when one puts Jesus first, others next, then yourself last, that JOY is found'. This follows the Maker's instructions in the Great Commandments, which can be summarised as 'love God and love others as you love yourself'.

MAYBE TODAY is a day for remembering that it's not *my* Christmas at all, but Jesus'. He's the One who said, '… Freely you have received, freely give' (Matt. 10:8). If you seek to be graciously selfless and radically generous, you will know true joy and blessing this Christmas.

PRAYER

Self-giving God, remind me today that there's more blessing in giving than receiving. In Jesus' name. Amen.

*Anagram answer: Tony Miles

BIBLE READING

THE GREATEST COMMANDMENT **Mark 12:28–34**
IT IS MORE BLESSED TO GIVE THAN TO RECEIVE **Acts 20:13–38**

FURTHER REFLECTION

Almighty God, from Your throne in glory,
You humbled Yourself and came alongside us.
You graciously kissed the earth of this fallen world.
You shone Your light into the dark places
through the precious gift of Jesus, Your Son, our Saviour.
Illumine our hearts, we pray, that softened by Your love,
we may, in humility, come alongside those in need.
Help us to reach out with compassion and generosity,
as channels of Your healing, peace, and hope.
May this be our gift to You, this Christmas,
for the sake of Your kingdom. Amen.

TM

SMILE

'What's another word for *thesaurus*?'

Steven Wright – comedian (1955–)

59 TREASURE IN HEAVEN

Christmastime can be expensive. Preoccupied by stretched budgets, we can forget our relative wealth. In Mark's Gospel we read that Jesus looked at the rich young ruler, "'One thing you lack," he said. "Go, sell everything you have and give to the poor, and you will have treasure in heaven. Then come, follow me'" (Mark 10:21).

Jesus knew the man's deepest need and 'loved him'. His gaze penetrated superficiality to the heart of the matter. Discipleship is more than religious observance! How much did the young ruler want to be a part of the coming kingdom? Well, he went away sad because he was more devoted to material things.

MAYBE TODAY is a day to reflect on your care for the poor and how you are influenced by materialism.

When I was first called to the Methodist ministry, I was living in Epsom, Surrey (a relatively 'well-off' suburban town). The Candidates' Committee asked me how I would preach on this text to stockbrokers in Epsom: 'Go, sell everything you have and give to the poor …'

It was a good question! My answer was that God wants everyone to be generous, but doesn't necessarily ask us all to give everything away. There's a challenge: would people be prepared to, if God asked? The young man wasn't, and that's why he walked away. The committee seemed happy with my reply. Jesus wants us to love Him in return and never seduced or persuaded anyone to follow Him. He always left decisions to individuals, whilst making it clear that He expects generous commitment from His followers.

PRAYER

Lord Jesus, help me not to put my trust in earthly treasure, but to store up treasure in heaven. Amen.

BIBLE READING

THE RICH YOUNG MAN **Mark 10:17–31**
WARNING TO RICH OPPRESSORS **James 5:1–6**

FURTHER REFLECTION

Who can tell what a day may bring forth?
Cause me therefore, gracious God,
To live every day as if it were to be my last,
For I know not but that it may be such.
Cause me to live now as I shall wish I had done when I come to die.
O grant that I may not die with any guilt on my conscience,
Or any known sin unrepented of,
But that I may be found in Christ,
Who is my only Saviour and Redeemer.

Thomas à Kempis – German monk and author of The Imitation of Christ
(1379–1471)

SMILE

'Christmas is when you buy this year's gifts with next year's money.'

Anon.

'24-hour banking? I haven't got time for that.'

Steven Wright – comedian (1955–)

60 IMPACT

One Christmas, Daniel, my production assistant for the *Big Breakfast* on Premier Christian Radio, gave me a calendar as a gift. I was reminded of his thoughtful gift as I had to take it down when the end of the year arrived. Each month displayed pictures of the Fulham FC squad. As an avid Fulham supporter, I was very pleased with it and had to order a replacement before the months rolled on through another year.

Now, I appreciate a Fulham calendar may have more of an impact on me than on you. However, there is a sense that all calendars should have an impact on us as we turn the pages. After all, we count our years roughly from the birth of Jesus Christ and our lives are ticking on. Even non-believers mark time by calendars, many of whom will admit that Jesus has left a lasting impression on the world. A New Testament scholar, C.D.F. Moule, commented: '... The size of the crater usually indicates the force of the explosion ...'

MAYBE TODAY you could consider whether you've let Jesus make an impression on your daily life and not just your calendar. Do people look at you and ask, 'What is it that's had such an impact on this person's life; what makes them live as they do? To which you reply, 'It's not what, but Who?'

PRAYER

Lord of the years, make an impression on my life today, so others will know I'm on Your side! Amen.

BIBLE READING

THE SUFFERING SERVANT **Isaiah 53**
ABRAHAM – A MAN WHO MADE A BIG IMPACT **Hebrews 11:8–19**

FURTHER REFLECTION

A prayer for a new year
God of the ages,
You are before us,
with us and beyond us.
Lead us, we pray,
from winter to spring;
from night to day;
from darkness to light;
from slumber to consciousness;
from an old year to a new beginning.
May Your renewing Spirit burst forth into our lives
with forgiveness, fresh vision, and blessed hope;
through the resurrecting power of our Lord Jesus Christ.
Amen.

TM

SMILE
'These are the good old days. Just you wait and see.'
Steve Turner – English music biographer, journalist and poet (1949–)

61 SELF-DENIAL

Lent begins on Ash Wednesday. It is a time for spiritual reflection. For many this includes giving something up – often food.

I recently came across this quote by Kenneth Collins: 'Today the word "fasting" means a total abstention from all food. In historic Christianity, it means a disciplined diet so that your animal appetites become a sort of spiritual snooze alarm.'[1]

I find that helpful. The idea is that when Christians discipline themselves during Lent, they harness their 'animal appetites' as a tool to wake them from their spiritual slumber. When the hunger pains come, it's like a 'snooze alarm' that kicks in to remind us to turn to God in prayer and devotion – to do business with God through repentance and faith. Throughout Lent it kicks in again and again.

MAYBE TODAY is a day for planning what you will secretly give up until Easter Day. It could help prevent you from sleepwalking in the faith. Whether you are giving up food, coffee, alcohol, the TV, magazines, cigarettes, or whatever, let abstinence lead you to God's Word and prayer.

PRAYER

Gracious God, during this holy season of Lent, may self-denial lead me to a deeper experience of Jesus. Amen.

BIBLE READING

JESUS' FORTY DAYS IN THE WILDERNESS **Matthew 4:1–11**
CREATE IN ME A CLEAN HEART **Psalm 51**

FURTHER REFLECTION

Grant, we beseech thee, O Lord, that by the observance
of this Lent
we may advance in the knowledge of the mystery of Christ,
and show forth his mind in conduct worthy of our calling;
through Jesus Christ our Lord.

*Gelasian Sacramentary – an ancient book of the Roman Catholic Church, written
by Pope Gelasius, and revised, corrected and abridged by St Gregory (5th century)*

SMILE

Minister: So, what are you going to give up for Lent?

Child: Sunday School!

TM

62 THE ROAD TO GLORY

Once when driving into London, I was struck by a large advertisement for sport on TV. It showed three footballers, including David Beckham, with the caption: 'Follow the road to Glory.'

On hearing the word 'glory', fame, wealth and success may come to mind. The 1966 World Cup was a glorious moment for English football, for example. Everyone wants to be on the winning side and to celebrate triumphantly, for we don't like trouble or defeat, and we're impatient when the going gets tough.

Yet, the apostle Paul said, we share in Jesus' sufferings 'in order that we may also share in his glory' (Rom. 8:17b). His words were very relevant to the many Early Church Christians who were suffering and dying for following Christ's 'road'. We also find this biblical principle in 1 Peter 4:13: '... rejoice that you participate in the sufferings of Christ, so that you may be overjoyed when his glory is revealed.'

MAYBE TODAY you'd do well to remember that just as Jesus was glorified through His death and resurrection, so obedient followers today will in time be glorified too. What's more, it will far outweigh your present afflictions. Christianity doesn't insure us against trouble. However, if you follow Jesus' way with faith, ultimately you will find that all is well! For true glory isn't a reward for suffering, but its fruit.

PRAYER

Lord Jesus, when suffering comes, may I remember that it's only temporary compared to the everlasting glory of Your kingdom. Amen.

BIBLE READING

LIFE THROUGH THE SPIRIT **Romans 8:1–17**
SUFFERING FOR BEING A CHRISTIAN **1 Peter 4:12–19**

FURTHER REFLECTION

Come, thou everlasting Spirit,
Bring to every thankful mind
All the Saviour's dying merit,
All his sufferings for mankind:

True recorder of his passion,
Now the living faith impart,
Now reveal his great salvation,
Preach his gospel to our heart.

Come, thou witness of his dying;
Come, remembrancer divine,
Let us feel thy power, applying
Christ to every soul, and mine.

Charles Wesley – hymn-writer, poet, evangelist and co-founder of the Methodist movement with his brother, John (1707–1788)

SMILE

'I definitely want Brooklyn to be christened, but I don't know into what religion yet.'

David Beckham – English footballer (1975–)

63 ETERNAL LIFE

I used to enjoy Scout camp. Yet, after a damp week under canvas, I'd be exhausted and ready to return home – a secure dwelling place.

Paul likened our bodies to tents! They are temporary dwelling places for our lives on earth. After the trials and joys of spiritual camping, we discard our bodies when we die, and put on heavenly clothes. With faith, we die and rise with Christ and find a secure resting place. No wonder Jesus said, 'In my Father's house are many rooms; if it were not so, I would have told you. I am going there to prepare a place for you' (John 14:2).

Death is the most certain fact of life for everyone. No one has to ask the question, 'Is there death after life?' But we should consider, 'Is there life after death?' A young woman once said, 'Well, I don't believe in heaven or hell, so therefore I won't be going anywhere.' The trouble is, not believing in something doesn't change its reality.

Christians have a tremendous message of hope beyond the grave. This doesn't take away the inevitability of death, or the pain of bereavement. Rather, faith in Jesus turns fear and trembling into faith and confidence. Someone once said that death is no longer 'a miserable cul-de-sac, but a glorious open road into the presence of God'.

MAYBE TODAY you could consider what a difference a resurrection faith makes to the way you live your life now.

PRAYER

Thank You, Jesus, for saying, 'Peace I leave with you; my peace I give to you. I do not give to you as the world gives. Do not let your hearts be troubled and do not be afraid' (John 14:27). Amen.

BIBLE READING

OUR HEAVENLY DWELLING **2 Corinthians 5:1–10**
IN MY FATHER'S HOUSE ARE MANY ROOMS **John 14:1–6,27**

FURTHER REFLECTION

When heaven's arches ring,
And her choirs shall sing,
At thy coming to victory,
Let thy voice call me home,
Saying, 'Yet there is room,
There is room at my side for thee!'
And my heart shall rejoice, Lord Jesus,
When thou comest and callest for me.

Emily Elizabeth Steele Elliott – hymn-writer and a niece of Charlotte Elliott, author of the hymn, Just as I Am. *(1836–1897)*

SMILE

Sign outside a church:
'Taking reservations for eternity. Smoking or Non-Smoking.'

Anon.

FOLLOW THE SUN (SON)

*Christine Watts writes: This is inspired by the fact that
sunflower heads follow the sun and it is in the style of
a Japanese Haiku – a minimalist form of poetry about
nature, which does not rhyme, and shouldn't have a
title. The idea is to say what you need to say in seventeen
syllables, usually in three lines each of five, seven and
five syllables. It's impossible for me to say anything in
seventeen syllables, so this is why it has eight verses!*

One seed sown, bursting
from the dark black feeding ground.
Tall stem waves, leaves dance.

Golden petals stretch
halo form round seed filled heart,
new life close embraced.

To follow the sun,
east to west, is daily work
for growth and glory.

Soon comes russet death,
embraced new life releasing
harvest abundance.

To follow the Son
is my daily work, my call,
life long joyful choice.

His the seed of love
which burst in my life, growing,
glorious and good.

His the crown of thorns,
sharp halo around my heart,
new life close embraced.

When sure my death comes,
may what I have been show too
harvest abundance.

EVEN MORE RANDOM

64 MINISTRY OF THE UNNAMED

Can you name the twelve disciples? Don't worry! Most people struggle. It's only 'show offs' who will list thirteen or fourteen men! It's not that their maths is bad, simply that the biblical lists aren't all the same – some disciples may have answered to different names. Some characters easily spring to mind, like Simon Peter, the brothers James and John (sons of Zebedee), Matthew Levi, doubting Thomas and Judas Iscariot. Yet, that's only half of them! There's also Andrew (Peter's brother), Philip, Bartholomew (who is possibly Nathanael), Thaddaeus (possibly also Judas son of James), Simon the Zealot/Cananean, and lastly, James son of Alphaeus.

Consider what's known about James son of Alphaeus. Precious little actually! We know more about some disciples than others. Yet, they were all apostles ('sent ones') and part of what became a dynamic group. They didn't all stand out in the crowd, proving it's not just prominent people who are important to Jesus. He uses and equips all whom He calls. This means that Christians should value each other, regardless of status. They should be comfortable with who they are in Jesus, and not try to be someone else – unless Jesus is changing them.

MAYBE TODAY you could pray for what's been called 'the ministry of the unnamed'. Some of the most powerful acts of Christian witness are in the quiet and unseen gestures. These Christian servants may not be preachers or leaders; they may not hold this or that office; nor are they credited or applauded for what they do. Nevertheless, they serve quietly, prayerfully, powerfully, and often anonymously. They have something to teach us about humility, and how to give the glory to God effectively.

PRAYER

Servant King, help me to encourage today those who serve faithfully and quietly and often without recognition. May I bless them and learn from them too. Amen.

BIBLE READING

WHO IS THE GREATEST? **Luke 22:24–30**
THE PHARISEE AND THE TAX COLLECTOR **Luke 18:9–14**

FURTHER REFLECTION

O God, in whom nothing can live but as it lives in love,
grant us the spirit of love
which does not want to be rewarded, honoured or esteemed,
but only to become the blessing and happiness of everything
that wants it;
love which is the very joy of life,
and thine own goodness and truth within the soul;
who thyself art Love, and by love our Redeemer, from eternity
to eternity. Amen.

William Law – the English spiritual writer and mystic (1686 –1761)

SMILE

There is a story about four people who were named Everybody, Somebody, Anybody and Nobody. There was an important job to be done and Everybody was sure that Somebody would do it, but Nobody did it. Somebody got very angry about that, because it was the job of Everybody. Everybody thought Anybody could do it, but Nobody realised that Everybody wouldn't do it. It ended up that Everybody blamed Somebody when Nobody did what Anybody could have done.

Anon.

65 UGLY FRUIT

Did you know that 'ugly fruit' are to make a comeback to the shelves in some supermarkets? In other words, misshapen strawberries, tomatoes, bananas, pears and the like, that usually get left behind, are to be on display once again. In the past they were deemed 'not good enough' for the British consumer. However, people now realise that 'while beauty might be skin deep', flavour certainly isn't.

If this is true for good old 'fruit 'n' veg', then how much more as far as people are concerned! We come from a variety of races and in all shapes, sizes and colours. It's all too easy to judge people by just looking at them, and perhaps comparing them to ourselves. What's more, the media constantly presents us with images of perfection in the form of models and superstars. If we are not careful, we can believe that we should be like that too.

MAYBE TODAY is a day for remembering that God isn't interested in external things, but He sees people from the inside – that's where real beauty should be. You can't hide from God, or pretend to be better than you are. He knows, and is not interested in face lifts or tummy tucks!

PRAYER

All-seeing God, forgive me those times when I judge a book by its cover, and help me by Your Spirit to nurture an inner beauty, in Jesus' name. Amen.

BIBLE READING

THE LORD LOOKS ON THE HEART **1 Samuel 16:1–13**
THE MESSIAH WON'T JUDGE BY SIGHT **Isaiah 11:1–9**

FURTHER REFLECTION

'Things which matter most must never be at the mercy of things which matter least.'

Johann Wolfgang von Goethe – German poet, playwright, novelist and philosopher (1749–1832)

'Beauty is truth, truth beauty – that is all.'

John Keats – English Romantic poet (1795–1821)

SMILE
'If God had meant them to be lifted and separated, He would have put one on each shoulder.'

Victoria Wood – comedian, actor, singer and writer (1953–)

66 THE FUTURE

It was Woody Allen who once asked: 'What makes God laugh?' His answer: 'Telling Him your plans for the future!' I smile, even though I've heard it so many times, for I'm one who likes to plan ahead – a typical Methodist! Yet, my experience in life is teaching me that only one thing is certain, and that is that the future isn't certain in this life.

Rabbis have a proverb: 'Care not for the morrow, for ye know not what a day may bring forth. Perhaps you may not find tomorrow!' That rings true for me: three members of my family from one generation have died unexpectedly in their fifties. We don't know what's around the corner and it's probably best that way. So why not consider how you can make the most of the life you've been given?

MAYBE TODAY you could invest in the present, rather than relying on the future; enjoy the moment and pay attention to your relationships – with your loved ones and especially with the Lord of eternity; don't put off until tomorrow that which can easily be done today!

PRAYER

Eternal Lord, You are the Alpha and the Omega (the beginning and the end). Though I don't know what the future holds, I thank You that I can trust that ultimately You hold the future. Amen.

BIBLE READING

THE PARABLE OF THE RICH FOOL **Luke 12:13–21**
THE NEW JERUSALEM **Revelation 21**

FURTHER REFLECTION

This, this is the God we adore,
Our faithful, unchangeable friend,
Whose love is as great as his power,
And neither knows measure nor end:

'Tis Jesus, the first and the last,
Whose Spirit shall guide us safe home:
We'll praise him for all that is past,
And trust him for all that's to come.

Joseph Hart – preacher and hymn-writer (1712–1768)

SMILE

'The future is something which everyone reaches at the rate of sixty minutes an hour, whatever he does, whoever he is.'

'There are two kinds of people: those who say to God, "Thy will be done," and those to whom God says, "All right, then, have it your way."'

C.S. Lewis – scholar, novelist, and Christian apologist (1898–1963)

67 PREOCCUPIED

It's surprising how many people forget to switch on their car headlights when pulling away on a dark winter's evening. On one occasion, I was following such a motorist in slow-moving traffic. All the way along the High Street I flashed my headlights in order to alert the driver concerned. Nevertheless, he was so preoccupied, looking out of the window, reading and adjusting his radio, that he failed to notice he was in danger.

The fact is, it's easy to become so preoccupied or carefree that you don't realise that you're travelling in the dark. Following the light of the person in front isn't good enough. Everyone needs personal illumination if they are to avoid the consequences of potential hazards.

MAYBE TODAY you should be careful to ensure your spiritual journey is in the light of Christ and that you're not blindly following others. However, fellow travellers may have something to teach you, but you'll only notice their signals and discern their relevance if you pay close attention.

PRAYER

Light of the Ages, help me to steer carefully and be ever vigilant. May I anticipate darkness along the road today. Amen.

BIBLE READING

JESUS, THE LIGHT OF THE WORLD **John 8:12**
WALKING IN THE LIGHT **1 John 1:5–10**

FURTHER REFLECTION

You are the peace of all things calm
You are the place to hide from harm
You are the light that shines in dark
You are the heart's eternal spark
You are the door that's open wide
You are the guest who waits inside
You are the stranger at the door
You are the calling of the poor
You are my Lord and with me still
You are my Love, keep me from ill
You are the light, the truth, the way
You are my Saviour this very day.

A prayer from Celtic oral tradition (1st millennium)

SMILE

For theological reasons, this minister finds it difficult praying for trivial things like a parking space. I feel God has far more important things to do. My wife, however, doesn't have such theological scruples and prays for a space if she really needs one. The annoying thing is, that I rarely find a space and she usually does!

TM

68 GROWING FOR JESUS

In our first book *Like a Child*, my wife Frances and I recalled my son's words when he was just three. As his mum's birthday was approaching, Jonathan said, 'Thirty-two is very big, Mummy … it's like up to the ceiling!' Well, you can understand where he got the idea. From a child's viewpoint you get taller with age. If it's true when you're three, then it must be true when you're thirty-something. By that reckoning, the very elderly Noah would've had his head sticking out of the ark, and the oldest man in the Bible, Methuselah, must've been an absolute giant by the time he died aged 969![1]

Each birthday is an exciting milestone in a child's life, especially when measured on a height chart. Adults, however, tend to try and forget how many times they've heard 'Happy Birthday' sung to them. Yet every year is a precious gift from God and *growth* is important. Birthdays are opportunities for asking, 'Am I still growing?' Not upwards, or outwards, but inwardly … spiritually! Such growth is often likened to a journey.

MAYBE TODAY, regardless of whether it's your birthday or not, you could reflect on your life's journey. What are you making of it? Where is your life heading? Howard Booth wrote, 'During the depression in Ireland they began to build roads to give the people something to do. They built roads out of towns and villages they believed would be built one day. But that day never came! They became 'ghost roads' which led nowhere.'[2] As the years pass by, be sure you are not wandering unconsciously into a spiritual cul-de-sac.

PRAYER

*Lord of the years, set my heart on a pilgrimage of faith that has a
sure destination. Amen.*

BIBLE READING

THIRTY-TWO IS NO AGE! **Genesis 5:21–32**
ADVICE FOR YOUNG AND OLD **Titus 2:1–8**

FURTHER REFLECTION

Lover of my soul,
may every day, every hour,
every minute, every second,
lead me closer to You
and to a deeper experience of You in my life. Amen.[3]
TM

SMILE
'Everyone has birthdays ... even grandads!'

Hannah Miles – my daughter (aged 4)

69 SPORT

In about 400 BC, the Greek philosopher Plato said, 'Sport is where men become as gods.' Sporting heroes are still among the idols of our generation – just consider the fuss about David Beckham moving to LA Galaxy in the USA. Similarly pop stars: Madonna and the so called 'king', Elvis.

Now it's okay to admire their talents and achievements, but should they become so lifted up they're touching the clouds? It's so easy for the mighty to fall and for their fans to feel let down. Life is unpredictable, fragile, and easily corrupted by pride and greed. It was Jesus who said, 'Happy are those who are humble; they will receive what God has promised' (Matt. 5:5, TEV).

MAYBE TODAY whether you're a sporting or pop hero, or just a fan, you can avoid disappointment by keeping two feet on the ground and by seeing Jesus as your role model. Sport may be where 'men become as gods', but *humility* is when God becomes a Man.

PRAYER

Heavenly King, thank You for all that is good in music and sport, but fill my star-struck heart with Your Spirit of humility and simplicity, that I may reflect the glory of Jesus. Amen.

BIBLE READING

QUITE A RECOMMENDATION **Numbers 12:3**
JESUS' HUMILITY **Philippians 2:1–11**

FURTHER REFLECTION

Lord, take as your right,
and receive as my gift,
all my freedom, my memory,
my understanding and my will.
Whatever I am and whatever I possess,
you have given to me;
I restore it all to you again,
to be at your disposal,
according to your will.
Give me only a love for you,
and the gift of your grace;
then I am rich enough,
and ask for nothing more.

St Ignatius of Loyola – Spanish founder of the Jesuits (1491–1556)

SMILE

'Some people believe football is a matter of life and death.
I'm very disappointed with that attitude. I can assure you
it is much, much more important than that.'

Bill Shankly – one of England's most successful football managers (1913–1981)

70 KEEPING HOPE ALIVE

I'm a bit of a dreamer. I enjoy thinking about the present and pondering what might be – my vivid imagination helps! Dreaming can be useful and fun – especially if you do it prayerfully. I'm not talking about my yearning for Fulham FC to win the FA Cup. Rather, taking time to consider what God wants the world to be like and what I want from my life. I've found God challenging me when I muse in this way.

I admire those whose hopes have had a prophetic edge and made a difference – often only after they've died. Martin Luther King Jr. (1929–1968) is probably one of the most famous 'dreamers'. On 28 August 1963, from the steps of the Lincoln Memorial and during the March on Washington for Jobs and Freedom, King's words were a defining moment for the American Civil Rights Movement. They included, 'I have a dream that my four little children will one day live in a nation where they will not be judged by the color of their skin but by the content of their character'. Over forty years after his assassination, people are still celebrating the progress that has been made, whilst recognising that there's a huge amount still to do for King's dream to become a global reality. As I listened to Barack Obama's eloquent speech after being elected as President of the United States of America, I was reminded of King's words. His dream is becoming a reality, but there's still more dreaming to be done!

MAYBE TODAY you could take time to dream a dream, or simply to ask God to help keep your hopes alive. What is the longing of your heart for your life, your loved ones, your community and our world?

PRAYER

All-seeing God, may my dreaming help transform the nightmares of this world into the reality of Your glorious kingdom here on earth. Amen.

BIBLE READING

JOSEPH INTERPRETS PHARAOH'S DREAM **Genesis 41**
PETER QUOTES JOEL THE PROPHET **Acts 2:14–21**

FURTHER REFLECTION

In the rush and noise of life,
help us wait upon you, O Lord.
Within ourselves may we be still and know you to be our God.
Day by day let us rejoice in the light of your presence;
through Jesus Christ our Lord. Amen.

*William Penn – English Quaker and the founder of the colony of Pennsylvania
(1644–1718)*

'Without leaps of imagination, or dreaming, we lose the excitement of possibilities. Dreaming, after all, is a form of planning.'

Gloria Steinem – American journalist and feminist (1934–)

'Imagination is more important than knowledge.'

Albert Einstein – German-born American physicist (1879–1955)

SMILE

'Optimists are wrong as often as pessimists. But they have a lot more fun.'

Anon.

PETER'S CHARGE

'Do you love me?'
'You know I'm rather fond of you,
care about you.'
'OK then, look after your friends.'

Again: 'Do you love me?'
'I guess I do – why else would I
still be with you?'
'Right, tell your neighbours everything I've said and done.'

Again: 'Do you love me?'
Irritated: 'Yes Lord, you know I do!'
'Good. Now go to everyone, give them this love;
I will go with you, tell you what to say.
Go now while you're able, there will
come a time when you can no longer choose
to go or come, when others will lead you here
or there against your wishes but even then
I will remain faithful to you
and you will always love me, live for me.'

Lord, may I too hear you asking:
'Do you love me?'
And may I not hesitate:
'Yes Lord, I love you.'

ADDITIONAL PRAYER MATERIAL

MOTHERING SUNDAY

Caring God,
today we praise You for mothers past and present.
None would claim to be perfect,
but we give thanks
for their unconditional love and tender hearts;
for their concern for our welfare;
for their patience and devotion;
for their healing and strength,
for their energy and skills;
for their influence upon our lives;
for their hopes and dreams.
On this Mothering Sunday,
embrace them in Your arms.
Renew, refresh and bless them.
For in all good mothers and fathers,
we catch a glimpse of Your perfect love for us. Amen.

TM

AFTER AN ACT OF TERRORISM

Originally written on 11 September 2001 and used again after 7 July 2005

Eternal Father,
we are numb with disbelief
and horrified to see the recent depths of human depravity.
Our hearts cry out: Why?
To be honest, we don't understand
and find it difficult to accept that such an atrocity should be
allowed to happen.
Yet, crucified God,
we believe that You weep with us,
just as Jesus wept over Jerusalem and at the death of Lazarus.

We know that this tragedy was not Your will.
Surround Your fragile world with Your everlasting arms
and bring healing to all pain, and comfort to those who are
grief stricken.
God of resurrection, may evil be overcome by good,
and let us not lose hope, as we pray for peace and stability.
Guide the leaders of the world, of all religions and races,
that they may be shown how to respond justly, humbly, and
with mercy,
for the sake of the vulnerable and innocent,
through Jesus Christ our compassionate and loving Lord.
Amen.

TM

HEALING

O Heavenly Father, in these few minutes of quiet stillness,
I place myself and all my problems humbly before You
for your guidance and blessing.
Help me to empty my mind of all earthly thoughts
so that in this stillness
I may be conscious only of Your heavenly presence near me.
Let the warm glow of Your wonderful healing power come into me
lifting all pain and distress from body and mind,
enriching me with new life and energy
and giving me inner peace and calm serenity.
Whatever my duties now or in the future
I shall always turn to You for guidance and inspiration,
knowing that Your light will be shining on my path
to help me walk through the darkness of this world
in the way You would have me walk – with my hand in Yours.
O Heavenly Father, bless me with renewed courage, strength
and understanding
that I may faithfully serve You and do Your will in all things.
Through the meditation of our Lord, Jesus Christ. Amen.

Anon. - source unknown

BIDDING PRAYER

For a Carol Service

We gather at Christmastime as the people of God
to be reminded of the biblical account of our Saviour's birth.

As we meet together in fellowship,
We pray that the Word of God will speak to us
and that we will be inspired through preaching;
through the singing of carols;
through hearing sacred music together;
and through offering open-hearted prayers.

We come moved by the obedience of Mary and Joseph, to kneel
in adoration with the shepherds and magi,
and to offer the gift of our surrendered lives.

All this is for the One who was born in humility and
vulnerability, to save us from our independence, pride and the
power of sin.

Loving God, we thank You for giving Your Son
to save us from ourselves,
and to transform this fragile and damaged world.

Forgive our preoccupation with our own concerns;
forgive our apathy concerning You and our spiritual well-being;
forgive our neglect of the needs of the poor and needy of the
world;
forgive us in the name of Jesus,
who was born to die upon a cross to put us right with You, our
Maker.

By Your Spirit, as we worship together,
may the profound mystery of the incarnation fill us with
wonder for this holy season,

and may the eternal significance of the Christ-child fill our
souls with joy and peace;
for our Saviour's sake. Amen.

TM

BLESSINGS

Go in peace,
for you have been in communion with the Lover of all Souls.
Continue to live in His grace and mercy
with trust and obedience.
May the gracious blessing of God Almighty,
Father, Son and Holy Spirit,
be with you,
with those you love,
and those you ought to love,
this day and for evermore. Amen.

TM

PRAYERS TO REMIND US OF THE WORLD CHURCH

THE GRACE

From the Philippines

Suma-atin nawa ang pag-papala ng Panginoong Jesu-Cristo,
ang pag-ibig ng Dios at ang pakikipag-isa ng Espiritu Santo
ngayon at mag-pakailan man. Amen.

THE PEACE OF GOD WHICH PASSES ALL UNDERSTANDING

From Ghana – Nhyira (Fanti)

Nyankopon asomdwee a otra
ntseasee nyina no onkora hom
akoma nye hom adwen wo
Nyankopon nye Ne Ba Jesus Christ hen Ewuradadze
ho nyimdzee nye do mu: na Otumfo Nyankopon Egya,
Oba, nye Sunsum Kronkron
No Ne nhyira no ombra hom mu na onka hom nyken daa.
Amen.

NOTES

INTRODUCTION

1. Philip Yancey, *What's So Amazing About Grace?* (Michigan: Zondervan, 1997) p.70.
2. Paul Valler, *Get A Life* (Nottingham: Inter Varsity Press, 2008) p.165.
3. Major W. Ian Thomas, *The Saving Life of Christ and The Mystery of Godliness* (Michigan: Zondervan, 1988).
4. Eugene H. Peterson, *Christ Plays in Ten Thousand Places* (London: Hodder and Stoughton, 2005) pp.44–45.

THE PACE OF LIFE

1. David Allen, *Getting Things Done* (London: Piatkus Books Limited, 2005) p.18.
2. Marcia K. Hornok, *Discipleship Journal* Issue 60, November/December 1990, p.23.

REACHING OUT

1. Tony & Frances Miles, *Like A Child* (Loughton: Rooftops Publishing, 2003) p.156.
2. As quoted in Ronald Brown, *Bishop's Brew* (London: Arthur James Book Publishers, 1993) p.17.

BREAKING BAD HABITS

1. Richard J. Foster, *Money, Sex & Power* (London: Hodder & Stoughton, 1985) p.104.
2. Tony & Frances Miles, *Like A Child* op. cit., p.177.

ACTIONS SPEAK LOUDER

1. Patrick Parkinson, *Child Sexual Abuse and the Churches* (London: Hodder & Stoughton, 1997) p.256.
2. P.J. O'Rourke, *The Bachelor Home Companion* (Avalon Travel Publishing; 1st Atlantic Monthly Pbk. Ed edition 2000).
3. As quoted in: J. John, and Mark Stibbe, *A Box of Delights* (London: Monarch Books, 2001) p.39.

OUT OF THE COMFORT ZONE

1. Oscar Romero may have been quoting Bishop Helder Camaro of Recife, Brazil – Roman Catholic theologian and clergyman (1909–1990).
2. Jim Wallis, *Faith Works* (London: Society for Promoting Christian Knowledge, 2002) pp.53–54.
3. Tim Cooper, *Green Christianity* (London: Hodder & Stoughton, 1990) p.56.

GOD'S MYSTERIOUS PRESENCE

1. Each New Day *Christianity Today* (Vol. 38, no. 1.)

PRAYER AND PRAISE

1. Ronald Brown, *Bishop's Brew* op. cit. p.61.
2. Brother Lawrence, *The Practice of the Presence of God with Spiritual Maxims* (New Jersey: Spire Books a division of the Baker Publishing Group, 1981) p.30.
3. Ibid, p.90.
4. Ibid, p.29.
5. Ibid, p.11.

LEARNING TO LIVE GOD'S WAY

1. Desmond Tutu, *An African Prayer Book* (London: Image/Doubleday, 1995) p.135.

SEASONS

1. From Rev Kenneth W. Collins' website: www.kencollins.com

EVEN MORE RANDOM

1. Tony and Frances Miles, *Like a Child* op. cit. p.138f.
2. Howard Booth, *Healing Experiences* (London: The Bible Reading Fellowship, 1985) p.49.
3. Tony and Frances Miles, op. cit.

BIBLIOGRAPHY

Reference and other books also used for background reading,
or consulted to verify quotes and prayers:

Ashwin, Angela *The Book of a Thousand Prayers* (Michigan: Zondervan, 2002).

Batchelor, Mary *The Lion Prayer Collection* (Oxford: Lion Hudson PLC, 1992 and 1996).

Benedictine monks of St. Augustine's Abbey, Ramsgate *The Book of Saints* (London: Cassell, 1994).

Braybrooke, Marcus *1000 World Prayers* (Alresford: John Hunt Publishing Ltd, 2003).

Crystal, David (Editor) *The Cambridge Biographical Encyclopaedia* (Cambridge: Cambridge University Press, 1998).

Hymns and Psalms (Great Britain: Methodist Publishing House, 1993).

McKenzie, E.C. *14,000 Quips and Quotes* (Eastbourne: Monarch Publications Ltd, 1991).

Northumbria Community *Celtic Daily Prayer* (London: Harper Collins Publishers, 2005).

Partington, Angela (Editor) *The Oxford Dictionary of Quotations* (Oxford, New York: Oxford University Press, 1996).

Paterson, Robert *The Monarch Book of Christian Wisdom* (Monarch Publications, 1997).

Pepper, Margaret *The Pan Dictionary of Religious Quotations* (London: Pan Books Ltd, 1991).

SPCK Book of Christian Prayer (London: Society for Promoting Christian Knowledge, 1995).

Tutu, Desmond *An African Prayer Book* (London: Image/Doubleday, 1995).

Other books were consulted when the material was originally written
for broadcast, but not all sources were recorded at the time. This is a
collection and the content was not originally written for publication.

PEOPLE INDEX

TM = Tony Miles (Anthony D. Miles)

BIBLICAL INDEX

THE AUTHOR –
A SHORT BIOGRAPHY

Tony Miles is married to Frances and they have two teenage children, Hannah and Jonathan. He is a Methodist Minister who is part of the ministerial team at Methodist Central Hall, Westminster. He is also a Media Chaplain, supporting primarily commercial radio, including Premier Christian Radio. Tony is a broadcaster himself and has presented the Saturday breakfast show for Premier since October 1997. Currently the programme is 6am – 11am and called *The Big Breakfast* which Tony co-presents with Lizzie Crow.

Tony is a regular contributor to *Living Light* (published by the Nationwide Christian Trust) and, with his wife, Frances, wrote *Like A Child* which they published through Rooftops Publishing in 2003. He is a trustee of the Churches Media Council, the Christian Evidence Society, and the Chigwell Riding Trust for Special Needs. He is actively involved with many other organisations – including the Churches Advertising Network and the Essex Churches Media Group. Tony is committed to family life which includes encouraging Jonathan in his football and Hannah in her drama. He is a member of the Rotary Club of Loughton and Buckhurst Hill, and his interests include: popular music, holidays, writing, the theatre, Fulham Football Club, and keeping fit at a local gym.

Tony's web site is www.tonymiles.com

National Distributors

UK: (and countries not listed below)
CWR, Waverley Abbey House, Waverley Lane, Farnham, Surrey GU9 8EP.
Tel: (01252) 784700 Outside UK (+44) 1252 784700

AUSTRALIA: CMC Australasia, PO Box 519, Belmont, Victoria 3216.
Tel: (03) 5241 3288 Fax: (03) 5241 3290

CANADA: David C Cook Distribution Canada, PO Box 98, 55 Woodslee Avenue, Paris,
Ontario N3L 3E5. Tel: 1800 263 2664

GHANA: Challenge Enterprises of Ghana, PO Box 5723, Accra.
Tel: (021) 222437/223249 Fax: (021) 226227

HONG KONG: Cross Communications Ltd, 1/F, 562A Nathan Road, Kowloon.
Tel: 2780 1188 Fax: 2770 6229

INDIA: Crystal Communications, 10-3-18/4/1, East Marredpalli, Secunderabad – 500026,
Andhra Pradesh. Tel/Fax: (040) 27737145

KENYA: Keswick Books and Gifts Ltd, PO Box 10242-00400, Nairobi.
Tel: (254) 20 312639/3870125

MALAYSIA: Salvation Book Centre (M) Sdn Bhd, 23 Jalan SS 2/64, 47300 Petaling Jaya,
Selangor. Tel: (03) 78766411/78766797 Fax: (03) 78757066/78756360

NEW ZEALAND: CMC Australasia, PO Box 303298, North Harbour, Auckland 0751.
Tel: 0800 449 408 Fax: 0800 449 049

NIGERIA: FBFM, Helen Baugh House, 96 St Finbarr's College Road, Akoka, Lagos.
Tel: (01) 7747429/4700218/825775/827264

PHILIPPINES: OMF Literature Inc, 776 Boni Avenue, Mandaluyong City.
Tel: (02) 531 2183 Fax: (02) 531 1960

SINGAPORE: Alby Commercial Enterprises Pte Ltd, 95 Kallang Avenue #04-00,
AIS Industrial Building, 339420. Tel: (65) 629 27238 Fax: (65) 629 27235

SOUTH AFRICA: Struik Christian Books, 80 MacKenzie Street, PO Box 1144,
Cape Town 8000. Tel: (021) 462 4360 Fax: (021) 461 3612

SRI LANKA: Christombu Publications (Pvt) Ltd., Bartleet House, 65 Braybrooke Place,
Colombo 2. Tel: (9411) 2421073/2447665

TANZANIA: CLC Christian Book Centre, PO Box 1384, Mkwepu Street, Dar es Salaam.
Tel/Fax: (022) 2119439

USA: David C Cook Distribution Canada, PO Box 98, 55 Woodslee Avenue, Paris, Ontario
N3L 3E5, Canada. Tel: 1800 263 2664

ZIMBABWE: Word of Life Books (Pvt) Ltd, Christian Media Centre, 8 Aberdeen Road,
Avondale, PO Box A480 Avondale, Harare. Tel: (04) 333355 or 091301188

For email addresses, visit the CWR website: www.cwr.org.uk

CWR is a registered charity – Number 294387

CWR is a limited company registered in England – Registration Number 1990308